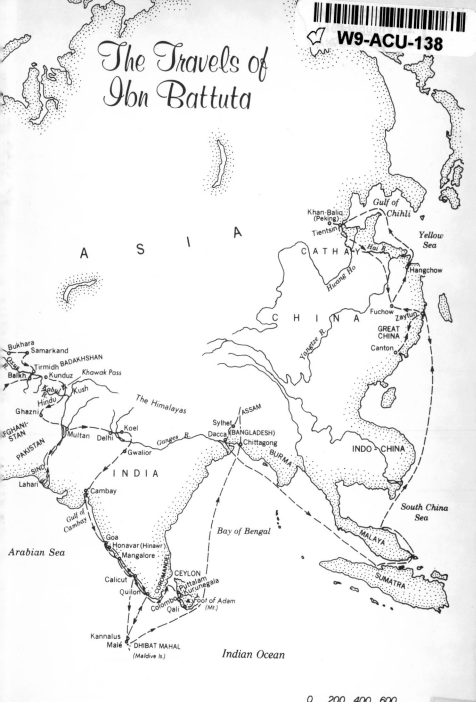

The Travels of Ibn Battuta

ASIA

CATHAY

Gulf of Chihli

Khan-Baliq (Peking)
Tientsin
Hai R.
Yellow Sea
Hangchow

Hwang Ho

CHINA

Yangtze R.

Fuchow
Zaytun
GREAT CHINA
Canton

Bukhara
Samarkand
Tirmidh BADAKHSHAN
Balkh
Kunduz
Khawak Pass
Oxus R.
Kabul R.
Hindu Kush
Ghazni
AFGHANI-STAN
PAKISTAN
SIND
Lahari

The Himalayas

Multan
Delhi
Koel
Gwalior

Ganges R.

Sylhet
ASSAM
Dacca (BANGLADESH)
Chittagong
BURMA

INDO-CHINA

INDIA

Cambay
Gulf of Cambay

Arabian Sea

Goa
Honavar (Hinawr)
Mangalore
Calicut
Quilon

COROMANDEL

CEYLON
Puttalam
Kurunegala
Colombo
Qali
Foot of Adam (Mt.)

Bay of Bengal

South China Sea

MALAYA

SUMATRA

Kannalus
Malé
DHIBAT MAHAL
(Maldive Is.)

Indian Ocean

0   200   400   600
Scale of Miles

THE ARAB
MARCO POLO: IBN BATTUTA

THE ARAB
MARCO POLO:
IBN BATTUTA

LUCILE McDONALD

THOMAS NELSON INC., PUBLISHERS
Nashville   New York

First edition

Library of Congress Cataloging in Publication Data

McDonald, Lucile Saunders.
    The Arab Marco Polo, Ibn Battuta.

    SUMMARY: A biography of the fourteenth-century Muslim scholar who traveled from his native Tangier to India and China, several times through the Near East, and to black Africa.
    1. Ibn Battuta, 1304–1377—Juvenile literature. [1. Ibn Battuta, 1304–1377. 2. Voyages and travels—Biography] I. Title.
G93.I24M32   910'.92'4 [B] [92]   75–4651
ISBN 0–8407–6441–3

CONTENTS

THE ARAB
MARCO POLO: IBN BATTUTA

I
Great Days for a Muslim Traveler

It was only a year after the death of Marco Polo—the Venetian who was the first to bring knowledge to Western Europe of China and the Far East—that a young Arab, who had never heard of the Italian's travels, started on a journey that was actually to better them.

Muhammad Ibn Battuta was fortunate in setting forth at a time when Islam was the foremost power in the world, holding sway in two of the three known continents and providing facilities for travel such as have never been known under other circumstances to any class of people. The Muslim faith of that day has been likened to a great brotherhood binding distant nations together with a common language— the Arabic in which the Koran was written. In the fourteenth century the Crusaders had gone from the Middle East, the Mongol invasion had passed, and comparative peace reigned before the hordes of Tamerlane were due to come out of Asia and topple Muslim power in many places.

Throughout the Islamic world, receiving a guest was then held to be a great virtue in the eyes of God. Giving alms and respect for those who made the pilgrimage to the holy cities of Mecca and Medina were also part of the Muslim belief.

These precepts, so favorable for the Moorish adventurer, dated from the beginnings of Islam toward the end of the sixth century. Muhammad, henceforth known as the Prophet, was born in Mecca in A.D. 571, the posthumous son of a man of modest circumstances. As a youth he tended sheep for his uncle, and when old enough he entered the service of a rich widow, Khadijah, proprietress of camel-freighting caravans. He managed her affairs so well that she married him when he was twenty-nine and she was forty. He prospered and had leisure for meditation, for which he had already shown a great inclination. When he attained the age of forty, he was experiencing visions, and as he was of an intensely religious nature, his wife and friends interpreted his hallucinations as messages from God. This began his career as an apostle preaching against paganism, which he continued to do the remaining twenty-one years of his life.

After Khadijah's death he was persecuted by the Meccans, causing him and a disciple to flee to Medina in A.D. 622. This flight, called the Hegira, is the time from which the Muslims date their calendar—as Christians do from the birth of Christ.

According to legend, the Angel Gabriel, serving as the mouthpiece of God, revealed the Koran to Muhammad. The Prophet, being a man of no education, could not read or write, therefore the revelations were recorded in scattered fragments by various persons. Some were not written at first and were wholly in his memory. Many of the ideas were borrowed from Jewish, Christian, and Persian Zoroastrian beliefs. That is why Islam recognizes many Bible stories. The name "Koran" is derived from an Arabic word meaning "a reading" or "a collection." It came into existence in its present form in A.D 660. The 114 chapters are very short and are composed in the simple, forceful Arabic of the desert Bedouins, employing many rhythmic clauses.

Muhammad had achieved a considerable following before his flight, and he continued to gain converts. As his influence spread and he attacked pagan sects, he sponsored raids on caravans from Mecca in order to have a source of revenue. Eight years after the Hegira, he conquered the city of his birth and made the Kaaba the principal Muslim shrine.

The Islamic movement had grown to such an extent that Muhammad headed a conquering army, which was made up of fast-moving, mailed light-horsemen armed with lances and javelins. Once a people were defeated, they were forced to convert to the faith. He permitted no one to fight on his side who had not embraced Islam, but after he won fame as a campaigner, he did not lack followers. He sent emissaries ahead of his armies to notify sovereigns and potentates that he would promise safety if they became Muslim. His advice to the feuding Arab tribes was that they settle their differences and devote their energies to converting the world. After his death the Muhammadan conquests spread from the Arabian deserts through Persia, Syria, Egypt, and North Africa. They tore away parts of the Byzantine Empire in what is now the Near East and threatened Europe. All the time the Arab invaders were gaining strength through their wholesale conversions—adding the Turks, among others, to their armies.

Following Muhammad's death the leadership of the Muslim community passed to his principal friend and then on to other chosen successors, some of whom were descendants of the Prophet through his daughters. These men took the title of caliph and became rulers of the East, conducting the holy wars Muhammad had started. The campaigns were carried into the mountains of Central Asia, to the Oxus River country, Bukhara, the Indus River, the Caucasus, Sicily, and Spain. Muslim dominion reached its peak in the tenth century, and though the caliphate declined after that, the religion had a firm hold, and before the end of the thirteenth century some of the leaders of the Mongol invasion were converted. Another means of spreading Islamic beliefs was through the Arab control of sea routes to Africa and Asia and in the Indian Ocean.

Along with their conquests the Arabs in the Middle Ages cultivated scholarship and encouraged learning along certain lines. They took pride in their poets and geographical treatises, but their most important contributions were in mathematics and medicine. Algebra, logarithms, and the numerical system that became the basis of modern mathematics can be credited to them. They made studies in astronomy and concluded that the earth was round, and they knew a great deal about navigation. They wrote books on Arabic grammar, rhetoric, logic, theology, philosophy, and cosmography. They also developed an architectural style based on knowledge obtained from conquered artisans.

There was no separation of politics and theology in the Muslim world. Religious beliefs always came first. The Muslim creed holds that "There is no god but God [Allah]: Muhammad is his Prophet." Its acceptance implies belief in the holy books (the Koran and the Hadith, a collection of the Prophet's sayings), the angels, the prophets, the day of judgment, and God's predestination of good and evil. It calls for performance of prayers five times a day, a month's fast during Ramadan, the giving of alms, and making a pilgrimage to Mecca if one is able. The Muslim creed must be recited at least once in a lifetime with full understanding of its meaning. Before prayer a Muslim must wash feet, hands, ears and face, then turn toward Mecca and prostrate himself. This was done at dawn, midday, midafternoon, sunset, and the early part of the night. Among the prohibitions of the faith were usury, gambling, picturing the human figure, consuming carrion, pork, blood, and alcoholic beverages.

While the Arabs had their origin in the desert peoples of Mesopotamia, the Turks, whom they converted to Muhammadanism, were descended from nomadic barbarians of Central Asia. They claimed their lineage from Noah through the eldest son of his son Japheth. Their home was Turkestan, but many strayed down into the Arab countries and were exposed to the Muslim religion. Their rugged appearance and vigor pleased the Arab princes, and some Turks were enrolled in the caliph's bodyguard prior to A.D. 1000, when the grandson of an emir named Seljuk expanded the fortunes of his tribe. Leaving the country of the Oxus River, he conquered Persia and entered Baghdad. His followers in large bands quietly oozed into Armenia and down into the valleys of Asia Minor, each Seljuk chieftain creating a kingdom out of the lands he conquered.

These Turks fought a battle with the Byzantine emperor in 1071, defeated him and left Asia Minor open to Islam. The Seljuks endowed mosques, constructed lasting buildings, and brought in financiers and statesmen to run their dominions. However, their rule failed to endure when the Mongols overwhelmed the country.

Another influx was also destined to engulf them—the Ottoman Turks, adherents of Soliman Shah, a leader who fled from his tribal grazing grounds in Khorassan ahead of the Mongol hordes. He took with him about 50,000 followers who made their way into the eastern provinces of Asia Minor. Soliman was accidentally drowned, but his son Ertogrul carried on and his men came to the aid of the last illustrious Seljuk sultan in a battle with Mongol horsemen.

Ertogrul remained a faithful ally of the Seljuk sultan of Konia and was rewarded with a gift of lands at Ankara, which his son, Othman, inherited shortly before the journey of Ibn Battuta. When the sultan of Konia died, Othman's rise to power marked the beginning of the Ottoman Empire.

Ibn Battuta came along during the transition period. Soon after his travels Mongol raids put a stop to journeys to the East. The Mongol empire in China collapsed, and the door closed against foreign visitors. With the end of the fourteenth century accounts of Arab voyagers became rare and less informative. In another hundred years the Americas had been discovered and world attention shifted to the new continents across the sea.

II
Prophecies for a Pilgrim

"For always wandering with a hungry heart, much have I seen and known of cities, of men and manners, climates, councils and governments."

Muhammad Ibn Battuta was to write this many years later, but the vague desire was formulating in his mind as the youthful rider guided his horse along a well-beaten track leading out along the narrow tongue of land that lay in front of the city of Alexandria. He was going to see what remained of that second of the Seven Wonders of the Ancient World, the Pharos, prototype of all lighthouses that were to follow it.

The young traveler from Morocco was jaunty in his flowing white robe and free-falling turban cloth. Of medium height and sturdy build, he probably had the clear-cut features

15

of his Berber ancestors—light skin of deep suntan color, keen gray-brown eyes, regular nose, dark brown hair, and close-cropped beard, slightly pointed on the chin. He was rested from his long, hard ride across North Africa with the pilgrim caravan, and for the first time in nearly nine months he had an opportunity to go sightseeing and enjoy the novelty of being in the great Egyptian port city, about which he had read in the mosque school he attended in Tangier, his home, 2,100 miles away as the birds fly.

It was cool and pleasant out on this finger of land, with the Mediterranean Sea lapping on both sides. There was a mound at the end that, many centuries ago, had been an island, connected with a mole which silted up until it became an isthmus. On top of the hillock stood the structure Ibn Battuta had come to see, a bulky square stone building with one side in ruins. He dismounted and walked around it. Being curious, he measured the base with his hands outspread, counting 140 spans, or 105 feet, the length of a side. The wall was 10 spans, or 90 inches, thick.

Ibn Battuta stepped back and looked up. He could not guess the height (it was supposed to have been four hundred feet in ancient times). Way up there on top a fire had burned nightly for many centuries (since around 300 B.C.) to guide ships into the harbor. The door to the tower was above the level of the earth, and to reach it one had to go through a small building and across a plank bridge that could be withdrawn for protection. Inside the entrance was the lightkeeper's abode.

These features were impressed on Ibn Battuta's memory— he had an unusual ability to store away facts. Having fully satisfied his inquisitive mind and being unaware that he would be the last traveler to leave a description of the famous building, he sat down by the shore and gave himself over to reflection.

How would he ever reconcile his longing to wander with

the logical course that lay open to him on his return home once he had completed his pilgrimage to the holy cities of Islam? He had studied to be a kadi, a Muslim judge. This profession had been traditional in his family for several generations. His uncles were kadis, and they had been in Tangier continuously for years and were revered by the people.

In his secret heart Muhammad did not wish to become so settled in one spot. True, it had been a wrench when he had left his devoted parents and set out. Later there had been regrets when he traveled the lonely road across Morocco, Algiers, and Tunis.

From his perch at the tip of the sandy point of land, Ibn Battuta observed sailing vessels entering Alexandria. They reminded the young man of those he had watched as a lad coming into the bay of Tangier. It was Morocco's principal port, and lying as it did at the Strait of Gibraltar, it was almost at the outer edge of the known world.

Ibn Battuta was born in Tangier on February 24, 1304, and had spent his first twenty-one years amid its pleasant surroundings. Its narrow streets spread up the slopes around the harbor, rising like steps of a great amphitheater to the gardens and villas. On clear days one could look across the strait and see the coast of Spain. Just over the western hill lay the Atlantic Ocean.

When Muhammad was old enough to have access to the few hand-copied geographical books in the seminary's scant library, he learned what the Arab travelers had found out about the universe. It consisted of Europe, Asia, and Africa and was strung out in a vast rectangle surrounded by oceans. Although some scholars believed the earth was curved, they did not know how far the seas extended or if they had a dropping-off place. One Arab geographer had said that, although the earth was round like a ball, the half opposite to the known portions was unihabited. The Atlantic Ocean was called the Sea of Darkness or the Green Sea of Gloom. It was thought boats might be able to sail around Africa, but few had been far down its west coast. In the east the land extended much farther. Zanzibar, off the East African coast, had been visited, and geographers wrote of India, spice countries beyond the Red Sea, and mysterious Asian places from which the Mongols had come. Of the north almost nothing was known; it was merely a vast cold region about which many myths existed.

It was part of Muslim education to learn where Mecca was, so that one might always face in its direction to pray. Most other learning centered around the mosque. Ibn Battuta was taught to read from the Koran, reciting it aloud, and he learned to write the Arabic letters in which it was written. The law that was intended to be his profession was also studied from the holy book.

When he had completed his schooling, he told his father, "I am ready to make the pilgrimage."

It was the duty of any devout Muslim to visit the holy cities of Mecca and Medina at least once in his life, if he could so manage his affairs. Ibn Battuta wanted an early start. Abdallah, his father, encouraged the idea and supplied his son with a horse to ride and an ass to carry his necessities for the road, the rug and quilt he would need for sleeping, and his extra clothing. He required little money for expenses, for the Islamic faith taught hospitality and charity. Pilgrims were respected, and holy men, religious foundations, and rulers along the way would provide for them.

Ibn Battuta recalled how confidently he had set out on June 14, 1325. His mother was sad. "Ah, my son, we may never see you again," she grieved.

Her sentiment was contagious, and the young Moor, who had never been far from his parents before, was soon overcome with homesickness. It was extremely hot in midsummer, the road was more lacking in travelers than he had anticipated, he felt terribly alone, and when weeks later he joined companions, he caught a fever. He was then miserably ill, a stranger in Bougie on the Algerian coast.

"You should stay here until you recover," advised one of the merchants with whom he was traveling.

Ibn Battuta could not bear the thought of being left by himself and in such a poor little port.

"No," he vowed. "If God decrees my death, it shall be on the road with my face set toward Mecca."

"Then, if that is your resolve," the man replied, "sell your ass and your heavy baggage, and I shall lend you what you require. In this way you will travel light, for we must make great haste on our journey, for fear of roving Arabs on the way."

Ibn Battuta saw he had no other course. He hated to part with the ass and the comforts for the road, but he must accustom himself to uncertainties and a new way of doing things. It was true he had reached country overrun with nomads, and no one was safe from them outside walled cities. Staying with the merchant caravan was the only practical thing for him to do. However, he was not long in regretting having parted with his possessions, for he became travel worn and bedraggled from the hard riding and being caught in a rainstorm when the party made camp in a grove by a river outside the large walled city of Constantine (in present Algeria).

Next day the governor rode out to meet the merchants, and they said they had a pilgrim in their midst. They introduced the forlorn-looking youth, and the governor at once ordered his clothing washed and sent him a new headcloth of fine Syrian fabric. In one end were tied two golden dinars, the first alms Ibn Battuta received on his journey. The new turban cloth proved a blessing when he suffered a second attack of fever on the road. In desperation he used the big scarf to tie himself in his saddle for fear he should become weak and fall. He was determined not to be left behind.

The last part of his traveling had been easier, for in the city of Algiers a large pilgrim caravan was being organized. It was ready to start early in October. On learning that Ibn Battuta had recently been a law student, the leaders appointed him

19

their kadi, to pass judgment on any wrongdoing in the ranks. It had taken until April to reach Alexandria, and by then he had outgrown his homesickness and youthful timidity, gained confidence, and was eager to add to his store of knowledge.

While the caravan rested, he intended to search out the city's most noted holy men and discover what he could learn from them. As a young theologian, he enjoyed sitting at the feet of revered oldsters, being a good listener and absorbing what he could of their philosophy and the lore of their country.

With this resolve, Ibn Battuta took a last look around the Pharos and turned back to the city. There was a scholarly sheikh he had heard about, who invited him to spend three days as his guest.

Before Muhammad Ibn Battuta ended his visit, the recluse observed, "I see you are fond of traveling in foreign lands."

"Yes, I am," the Moor replied. Of course, he explained, his only purpose at present was to complete the pilgrimage.

The sheikh knew three learned men who had gone away to different places, two in widely separated parts of India and another to China. Naming them, he said, "You must certainly visit my brothers in faith in your travels and carry my greetings to them."

Ibn Battuta was baffled by this statement. Such countries were beyond his imaginings, places he had only vaguely heard of. He had been told that his host was noted for his gift of prophecy but would have brushed off the prediction of the old recluse except for something that happened a few days later.

Ibn Battuta rode out to Fuwa in the country east of Alexandria to visit a second pious sheikh, who was much consulted by princes and ministers. When he reached the small house beside a canal, he found he was not the only visitor. One of the sultan's aides-de-camp was there, and his troops had set up tents nearby.

The sheikh received Ibn Battuta with an embrace, fed him bountifully, and when night came, invited the young man to go up on the roof and sleep there, as it was extremely hot. Ibn Battuta found a leather mat and straw-filled mattress awaiting him. Before he wakened, he had a vivid dream. He was on the wing of a great bird flying toward Mecca, then to Yemen. After that the bird flew east, then south, then east again, and finally landed in a dark and green country, where it left Ibn Battuta. The dream was so strongly imprinted on the Moor's mind that he related it to the sheikh in the morning and asked, "What do you understand from it?"

"That is very clear," the holy man replied. "You will go on your pilgrimage and visit the tomb of the Prophet. Then you will travel through Yemen, Iraq, the country of the Turks, and India. You will stay there for a long time."

Ibn Battuta was gratified to hear this prophecy repeated, and his spirits went soaring. Two such predictions within a short time of each other, and from such respected personages, must have meaning.

If indeed these two old men were gifted with telepathic powers, they showed they understood Ibn Battuta's aspirations better than he did himself. He interpreted it that, when revered savants foretold such a course, he was being given divine guidance.

As he departed from Fuwa, his purpose was firm. He knew what he was going to do. Surely God intended that he should travel far and seek knowledge of as much of the world as possible before returning home.

But first he had a duty to perform—he must complete his journey to Mecca.

III
Mecca and Caravan Country

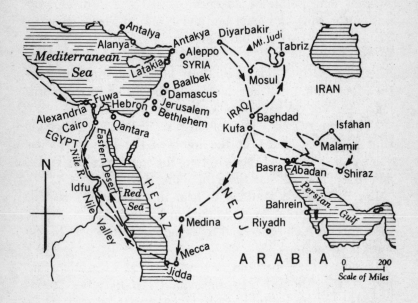

In the fourteenth century there were no shortcuts to travel. To reach Egypt Ibn Battuta had covered the entire winding circuit of the North African coast, then to go to Mecca he turned south toward the Upper Nile Valley, aiming to reach the Red Sea. At Idfu (about fifty miles north of the present Aswan Dam) the party he was with joined some Arabs and hired camels in preparation for spending fifteen days crossing the Eastern Desert. It was a trying journey, and he especially remembered the night hyenas attacked their camp. The travelers were up constantly, driving the animals off with sticks and stones. One got into Ibn Battuta's belongings and made off with a sack of dates.

When the pilgrims reached the shore of the Red Sea, they

would be only about 120 miles across the water from Hejaz and the terminus of the road to the holy city of Medina. They had brought provisions for the short voyage, and since the midsummer heat again prevailed, they were looking forward to reaching the oases of the Prophet's land.

Thus when their camels trooped into the large town on the shore from which they were to have departed, they regarded the scene in dismay. Instead of the vessels with slanting sails they had expected to find, there were no boats. The mystery of this port without shipping was soon explained. The black king who ruled that part of the coast was at war with the sultan of Egypt. All the boats had been sunk in the fighting or else had sailed away to safety.

Ibn Battuta had come so far to no avail, going out of his way for several weeks and enduring hardships in the desert heat. There was no way to get out except over the same camel route across the harsh sands. He and his companions talked among themselves and agreed that in its state of war this was no place to stay and wait. Reluctantly they sold their sea provisions and made the disheartening trip back to the Nile with the camelmen. After that Ibn Battuta could not get out of Egypt fast enough. The river was in flood, so he boarded a boat and sailed eight days downstream, landing in Cairo two months after he had left it. He remained only one night in the metropolis, although it was the biggest city he had ever seen, and in it, he later wrote, he was conscious of a boundless multitude of buildings and crowds surging like waves on the sea. He had already spent some days in Cairo on the up journey and absorbed statistics about its 30,000 mule and donkey drivers, 12,000 water carriers with camels, and the 36,000 boats on the river. He had seen enough and did not want to linger.

In those days the Egyptian-Syrian frontier was only a few miles from Qantara, close to where the Suez Canal now lies. Customs stations were located on the travel route, where taxes were collected from merchants, and travelers passing through had to present a passport from one country to the other. The authorities were most particular. They had the sand smoothed at night to obliterate tracks, and in the morning they inspected the route. If anyone had crossed in the darkness, he was pursued and punished.

Ibn Battuta's party was treated with kindness and went on up the coast through the cities of what is today Israel. Many of the spots that are revered for their biblical associations are also respected by Muslims. At Hebron Ibn Battuta carefully examined the sacred cave containing the graves of Abraham, Isaac, and Jacob and interviewed an aged professor of religious sciences to learn the truths about them. He visited the graves of Joseph and Lot, then went on to the birthplace of Jesus at Bethlehem, where the Christians hospitably welcomed all travelers who alighted at the shrine. Jerusalem was regarded as the third most holy city in Islam, for here the Prophet Muhammad was said to have ascended to Heaven. Ibn Battuta inspected the great mosque and the Dome of the Rock and the sanctuaries, both Muslim and Christian. He called on kadis, sheikhs, and professors and thoroughly enjoyed himself.

Having decided to see all he could, he spent some weeks going up the Lebanon coast as far as Antakya (the European Antioch, in present Turkey) and Aleppo (in present Syria). In addition to gathering stories about Muslim heroes and saints, he liked wandering in the bazaars and observing how foods, sweetmeats, and various products were manufactured. When he turned inland and went back through Baalbek (in present Lebanon), it was not the ruined Greek temples of that city that attracted him but the marvels of woodworking. He reported:

They make here wooden vessels and spoons that have no equal in the world. They will make a large dish, then make a second one which fits into the hollow of the first, and

24

another in the hollow of that, and so on to as many as ten, which anyone seeing them would imagine to be a single dish. In the same way with spoons they make a series of ten, one within the hollow of the other, and make a leather covering for them.

You see, a man will carry this case in his belt and on joining in a meal with his friends will take it out. Those who see it think it contains a single spoon, whereupon he distributes nine others from within it.

Odd facts like these were stored away in Ibn Battuta's memory, to be brought out when he related wonder tales of his travels.

He reached Damascus on August 9, 1326, and took up lodging in a college, preparing to spend the rest of the month exploring the city until the pilgrim caravan was ready to depart for Hejaz on September 1. Damascus impressed him with its beauty from the moment he saw its white minarets rising above a surrounding field of verdure. He found that inside the high walls of its houses were lovely gardens. Streets were narrow, but they led to impressive buildings. The cathedral mosque (where today is the Church of Saint John) seemed to him the most attractive in the world.

The eastern portal, largest of the four entrances to the mosque, was called the Door of the Hours because to the right of it was an upper gallery shaped like a large arch and containing a rare sight. Inside this arch Ibn Battuta observed smaller ones with twelve doors painted green on the inside and yellow on the outside. They were parts of a mechanical water clock, the inside of one turning out and another closing as each hour passed. The Moor heard that a person in the room was responsible for turning them by hand, which may or may not have been true, as the doors could have been operated by a ratchet wheel. Water clocks were an elaborate invention and not many were in existence. This one probably had tanks, a column marked with the hours, a bar that rose on the side as the water dripped out, and a long wooden arm to control the wheel and turn the doors.

Another thing Ibn Battuta observed at the mosque was the way in which writing was taught. At first pupils sat on the floor around a teacher and heard him dictate from the Koran. They recited the lines back from memory but did not write them down on their tablets, lest they make mistakes and pollute the Book of God. When the memory work was completed, they went to another person who instructed them out of books of poetry and the like. Here they were taught calligraphy.

Ibn Battuta improved his own education while he was in Damascus, attending several series of lectures, where he sat crosslegged on a rug, listening to scholars explain holy books. He was extremely proud when in the space of twenty-two days he earned several diplomas and a general license to teach.

With his ability to make friends with learned men, Ibn Battuta was welcomed at the home of a religious professor and spent several nights in Ramadan with him. (Ramadan is the ninth month of the Islamic calendar, during which the faithful fast every day from sunrise to sunset.) On becoming ill again with a fever, the Moor excused himself and stayed away. The professor refused to hear of this, sending for the traveler and declaring, "Consider my house as your own, or as the house of your father or brother." He then summoned a doctor and ordered medicines and special dishes for the invalid.

Ibn Battuta's money ran out, and he was unable to buy provisions and rent camels to continue his pilgrimage. The professor, learning about his difficulties, supplied all that was necessary and thrust money upon the young man, insisting, "It will come in useful for anything of importance that you may be in need of."

The misfortune of being without any funds at all could not have overtaken Ibn Battuta in a better place, because there was no city like Damascus for aiding devout travelers and for helping others. Anyone reaching the end of his resources was always given a means of livelihood, employed as imam (or prayer leader) in a mosque, as reciter in a college, or as keeper of a sanctuary, or was simply handed an allowance so that no stranger need lose his self-respect. Damascus had remarkable endowments, such as one to supply wedding outfits to girls who could not afford them, others for feeding prisoners and for a variety of other charitable purposes.

One day Ibn Battuta was passing in a lane when he saw a small slave drop a Chinese porcelain dish, which broke in fragments. Among the persons who collected around him was a man who advised, "Gather up the pieces and take them to the custodian of the endowments for utensils."

The man offered to go with the young slave, and together the two left the scene. Ibn Battuta asked and was told that the slave would receive a sum sufficient to buy a similar dish, thus avoiding a beating or a scolding from his master.

"This benefaction is indeed a mender of hearts," he said.

Ibn Battuta was well recovered from his fever when the pilgrim caravan set out. It stopped outside a place called the Castle of the Raven at the edge of the desert and waited four days so that everyone would be ready for the crossing and all slow starters had caught up. After the last town in Syria (in present Jordan), he saw only sand and at great distances wells where water carriers camped. They had constructed cisterns of buffalo hides from which they watered the camels and filled the waterskins, being paid for this.

The Moor had been invited to travel with a band of Bedouin Arabs. It was necessary to journey day and night so as not to prolong the desert trip. Ibn Battuta heard stories of terrible years for the pilgrimage when there had been no water in the wells. After the worst part of the crossing, a stop was made at a pleasant village with palm gardens and springs, where the travelers washed their clothes. Three days later the caravan was on the outskirts of Medina, the holy city where the Prophet's tomb was located. It was an oasis in a

27

mountain basin and was surrounded by a well. On its eastern side rose the minarets and lofty dome of the great mosque. An imposing gate led to a deep portico with pillars, at the end of which was a chamber hung with rich curtains. Here the Prophet and two of his companions were interred.

This mosque was where Muhammad had preached from a wooden pulpit, and near it he had dwelt. It had begun as a humble sanctuary built of palm trunks and roofed with their leaves, but had grown and become an impressive building. There still remained a palm trunk against which the Prophet had stood when he preached.

When the pilgrims arrived, they went at once to the holy place, praying in the garden between the tomb and the pulpit and reverently touching the fragment of the tree. Then they filed past the tombs. Their stay in Medina lasted four days, and each evening they gathered in circles on the marble-paved courtyard of the mosque. Here, by the light of candles, they intoned litanies and recited the Koran from volumes set on rests in front of them.

The travelers were now ready to resume their journey to Mecca, which meant crossing a frightful desert for three days. This was rough going for Ibn Battuta. Five miles out of Medina he and all the others removed their travel clothing, bathed, and dressed in pilgrim garb, which consisted of two white cloths, one around the waist and one over the shoulders. This change of clothes was prescribed by custom for old and young and for men of all races. It was what the Prophet had done many years before.

Ibn Battuta rejoiced when at last a fruitful valley hove in sight. He was excited to be so near his goal that he forgot the dangers, fatigues, bad luck, and troubles he had undergone to get this far. God had granted him the privilege of completing his journey, and he reported afterward, "We set out at night from this blessed valley with hearts full of joy."

In the morning the great band of pilgrims arrived in the holy city and, as was their duty, immediately entered the courtyard of the principal mosque and began the required rite consisting of walking seven times around the Kaaba. This was the sanctuary that housed the most holy object in all Islam, the ancient black stone, probably a meteorite, that had been worshiped in pagan times. Muhammad had purged it of the taint of idols, and the story went that Gabriel gave it to Abraham, and he and Ishmael built the original temple there.

Without being told, Ibn Battuta knew what he could expect to find. The Kaaba stood by itself in the courtyard, a small square brown stone building with a door high off the ground. The entire structure was covered with a huge black silk brocade cloth embroidered around the bottom with inscriptions from the Koran. This cover was raised up so that the holy corners of the Kaaba were exposed. In the southeast corner was affixed the heavenly stone. Ibn Battuta squeezed his way through the jostling crowd of worshipers until he could reach up with his lips and kiss the holy object. Then he bowed and performed a prayer, touched the great curtain respectfully, and approached the nearby well of Zamzam to drink from its water. Each thing that he did had significance. Kissing the stone was a means of establishing mystic contact with the hand of God.

The happy pilgrim from Tangier went away exalted. In the ecstasy of reaching the holy place, he had not given thought to the scorching black pavement beneath his bare feet, but now he gratefully donned sandals and took nourishment in the shady confines of a nearby college.

In spite of the immense crowds in the city during the pilgrimage, he knew where to find hospitality. There were many other holy rites to perform and shrines close by to visit as well as saintly men to interview. Ibn Battuta left undone no duty a good Muslim pilgrim should discharge.

He had now made the Hajj, the holy pilgrimage to the most sacred shrine of Islam. Henceforth, he would be addressed as Haji, "one who had made the Hajj," a title of great respect.

When he had completed his religious obligations, it was

time to think of his future. Would he be as fortunate finding hospitality traveling away from Mecca as he had found coming toward it? A venerable philosopher might have expected it, but how about a young man of twenty-two? Well, he could only do as he had done, obtain the best introductions he could muster and put a bold face on his venture.

A caravan of pilgrims returning to Iraq, Iran, and Khorasan (today a region in eastern Iran) would be leaving soon, and he intended, if possible, to accompany it, for that would be taking the easiest direction he could follow if he was to carry out his intention of seeing more of the Muslim world. He contrived to be presented to the emir in charge of the expedition. Ibn Battuta must have had some very persuasive and winning qualities, for he made an agreeable impression at once on the great man. The latter generously hired half of a double camel litter as far as Baghdad for the young traveler and took him under his personal protection. The Moor was told to be ready to depart on November 17, 1326.

This was the largest caravan Ibn Battuta had yet seen, and he discovered immediately after starting that, if he left the litter for a few minutes' comfort stop, it would be difficult to return to his place without having found some mark to guide him in the immense throng.

In addition to the pilgrims' mounts, there were hundreds of extra draft camels to carry water, provisions, and medicines for those who fell ill. At mealtime halts, the food was cooked in huge brass caldrons, and some was dispensed to the poorer men who had brought nothing. The caravan went on marching in the night, its way illuminated by torches carried in front of the files of camels and litters. Ibn Battuta napped as they went along, but sometimes he would waken and observe the troop's shadowy progress across the desert in the flickering light.

The land of Nejd (the central region of the Arabian peninsula), through which they had set a northeastern course, was

level as far as eye could see. Every few days there were stops at ancient water tanks. Here Bedouins traded sheep, melted butter and curdled milk.

The caravan routine was interrupted at Kufa on the Euphrates River, where the pilgrims separated and went in different directions. Ibn Battuta decided to leave the main body and go downstream with a large company of armed Arabs bound for Basra. He was warned there were powerful and violent inhabitants in the region he must pass through and that there was no safety without guardians who were native to the country. He had to leave his comfortable litter with the main caravan and hire one of the Arabs' camels.

The travelers passed along the edge of a reed jungle in the delta, a saturated land that was inhabited by Marsh Arabs, noted as brigands. This was a lonely, desolate region, and Ibn Battuta was careful to stay close to his armed escort. A party of dervishes (members of a Muslim religious brotherhood) were not so cautious. They dropped behind. Suddenly renegades appeared out of the marsh and attacked them so quickly they were stripped of everything they carried, including their shoes and wooden bowls, before help could arrive. As speedily as they had come, the marauders disappeared and retreated to their fortified refuges deep in the maze of swamps.

For three fearful days the travelers traversed the country bordering the marsh, and it was a relief to approach the big city of Basra, at the head of the Persian Gulf. Outside it Ibn Battuta observed a mosque as lofty as a castle, which roused his curiosity. While he was stopping in Basra several days, he called on a distinguished sheikh, who showered him with gifts of hospitality, clothing, and money. The Moor went out to the tall mosque to attend Friday services and climbed one of its seven minarets to learn the truth of a story he was told. It was said that when certain invocations were voiced, the slender structure would shake. Ibn Battuta tried it out, and the minaret obliged him by quivering.

He was less pleased when he went inside the mosque and heard the preacher commit numerous errors of grammar during his discourse. Ibn Battuta complained to the kadi that this was unbelievable in a city noted as the place where the rules of Arabic grammar were written and the standards of correct classical usage were fixed. Here the art of grammar once had reached its height.

The kadi regarded him sadly and admitted, "In this town there is not a man left who knows anything of the science of grammar."

Ibn Battuta had a hard time reconciling this lapse with what he had been taught by his professors in the mosque schools.

A few days later he was in Abadan calling on a hermit. (Abadan, though only a few miles from Basra, is located across the river in present Iran.) The holy recluse took the Moor's hand at parting and earnestly said, "May God grant you your desire in this world and the next."

Ibn Battuta interpreted this as reaffirmation of his wish to travel far and wide. He made a new resolve that never, if he could help it, would he journey a second time over any road he had once traveled.

This accounted for his zigzag route in Iran during the next few months. He hired a horse and with a dozen companions headed into the Zagros Mountains. Wherever Ibn Battuta traveled, he contrived never to be alone, and this time he had joined up with an imam, two reciters of the Koran, and "other poor brethren." They found hospices at the end of each day's journey, where travelers could stay and were supplied with bread, meat, and sweets.

At Malamir (modern Izeh), capital of a small sultanate in northwestern Iran, Ibn Battuta, as was his regular custom, sought out a prominent and pious sheikh, who sent him to a hospice for lodging. The Moor wished to meet the sultan, but there were objections. The monarch's son was extremely sick, and the ruler went out only on Fridays when he prayed at the mosque.

"He does not receive visitors," Ibn Battuta was told. "One reason is that he is addicted to drinking wine."

This was contrary to the teachings of Islam. Two other indulgences were forbidden by the Koran—gambling and eating pork.

Word got around about the presence of the travelers, and a royal servant called on them, asked questions, and returned bearing two great platters. One contained food and the other fruit and a pouch of money. The servant evidently had mistaken Ibn Battuta's companions for dancing dervishes, and he requested them to dance and pray for the recovery of the ruler's son.

"We have no association with music and dancing," Ibn Battuta told him, "but we will pray for the sultan and his son."

He divided the coins among his companions. That night the sick boy died, and in the morning the sheikh came and insisted that Ibn Battuta go to the palace with a company of the city's principal men for a ceremony of condolence. The audience hall was filled with slaves, nobles, and soldiers all wearing sackcloth, putting dust and straw on their heads and beating their breasts and crying, "Our master!"

It was a strange sight, such as the Moor had never seen. He looked about for a place to sit and saw a small dais, in one corner of which was a lone man wearing a felt robe such as poor people donned on rainy days. Ibn Battuta went up, greeted him, and sat down on the opposite corner of the dais. He was startled to find everyone staring at him. A kadi signaled for him to come away. At this the traveler began to suspect he was sharing the dais with the sultan. He concluded it was best to remain where he was until the funeral service ended.

At its conclusion he had not yet said anything to the man in the felt cloak and did not know if his temerity in remaining

seated on the dais had vexed the monarch and he would be
punished. Several days passed, and the messenger who had
brought the trays reappeared with a command that Ibn Battuta visit the sultan at once. He could not surmise whether
his reception would be good or bad. He was escorted through
the streets to an impressive gate, taken up a long staircase and
into a large, unfurnished room. It was that way, the messenger
explained, because of mourning for the sultan's dead son.

The ruler sat on a cushion with two covered goblets in
front of him, one of gold and one of silver. A green rug
was spread nearby, on which Ibn Battuta was instructed to sit.
He was uneasy as he took the indicated place. Only the chamberlain and another man remained in the room with the king
and his visitor. The sultan spoke Arabic well. He appeared
to be in a friendly mood, but Ibn Battuta was not trustful.
There was something wrong about this king.

"Tell me about yourself and your country," the monarch
said. "I should also like to hear about the sultan of Egypt
and any news you have brought from the Hedjaz."

At that moment a doctor of law entered the room, and the
sultan's mood became maudlin. He spoke so foolishly that Ibn
Battuta concluded he was drunk.

The sultan saw that his visitor was disturbed.

"Speak what is in your mind," he ordered.

The Moor was never one to flinch. He risked affronting the
monarch again. Without fear he said, "If you will listen to me,
I say this to you: You are the son of a sultan noted for piety
and uprightness, and there is nothing to be brought against
you as a ruler but this." He pointed to the wine goblets.

The sultan reddened and said nothing.

Ibn Battuta knew he had given offense to his host and
asked permission to leave.

"No, sit down," ordered the sultan. "To meet with a man
like you is a mercy."

Since the ruler was in truth very drunk and seemed about

to fall asleep, Ibn Battuta made another move to withdraw. The doctor of law helped him look for his sandals, which it was customary to remove at the door during an audience.

"God bless you," the wise man told the traveler. "What you said to the sultan none could say but you. I hope this will make an impression on him."

Ibn Battuta expected some unpleasantness to result from the encounter. He wanted to leave Malamir at once, but he could not risk departing alone in perilous country. So while awaiting his companions, he anticipated an angry summons to the palace. The messenger arrived again, but there was no reason for alarm. He brought a farewell gift of money from the sultan.

Looking back on such happenings, it is incredible how early in his travels Ibn Battuta established himself as a person of consequence. To have risked a ruler's displeasure was dangerous in any era. Such was the temper of the times, however, that a truly devoted follower of the Muslim faith merited respect. Ibn Battuta had a persuasive quality about him, bolstered by the courage of his convictions, that carried him through alien lands unscathed.

He traveled as far as Isfahan and Shiraz (in present central and south-central Iran), then turned back toward Iraq. It was a long ride to Baghdad, a city of strange sights, among them bridges across the Tigris River made of continuous rows of boats chained together. The baths impressed him as curious, and when he described them he did not know he was telling of a substance that six hundred years later would be the key to the country's wealth. Here is how he recorded his first look at a petroleum product:

Baghdad has numerous baths, excellently constructed, most of them being painted with pitch, which has the appearance of black marble. This pitch is brought from a spring between Kufa and Basra, from which it flows continually. It gathers at the sides like clay and is shoveled up and brought to Bagh-dad.

In each of these bath houses there are a large number of cubicles, each floored with pitch and having the lower half of its wall coated with it, and the upper half coated with a gleaming white gypsum plaster. Every private room has a wash basin in the corner with two taps supplying hot and cold water. Every bather is given three towels, one to wear around his waist when he goes in, another to wear when he comes out and a third to dry himself with. In no other town have I seen all this elaborate arrangement.

When he had observed enough of the city to satisfy himself, Ibn Battuta joined the ruler's camp on purpose to see how royalty conducted marches. From being interested at first only in saints and scholars, he decided to go into the histories and lives of sultans on the way. Slowly he was perfecting a method for carrying out his design. Here in Iraq was an elaborate camp in which to commence his regal education.

On either side of the sultan traveled fifty principal emirs, color bearers, clarion players, and trumpeters, and after them his slaves. Each emir had his own standard bearers, trumpeters, and drummers. The cortege included the princesses followed by their baggage, and at the end of the procession marched the army. The barbaric pomp was unflawed by any disorder. Anyone dropping behind was punished by being obliged to make the rest of the journey barefoot over the hot sand to the next stopping place, where he was given a beating.

After ten days amid this splendid cavalcade, Ibn Battuta was satisfied with what he had observed and left the cortege with an emir bound for Tabriz, a great Persian trading city (in present northwestern Iran), which attracted merchants from the west. Its bazaar was dazzling. Ibn Battuta gaped in awe at the jewelers' stalls filled with precious stones. These dealers employed beautiful slave boys in rich garments to stand in front of the shops and put on the gems, exhibiting them to Turkish women who came to buy.

Rivaling the jewel market was the section where ambergris and musk perfumes were sold. Ibn Battuta was scandalized at seeing so much attention paid to satisfying vanity, and he could only exclaim over these two sections of the bazaar and their customers, "May God preserve us from such!"

He had been only a night in Tabriz when the emir was ordered back to the sultan's camp. Ibn Battuta went along, and on his arrival there he was introduced to the ruler, who generously supplied him with robes, a horse, and provisions. The Moor had decided to make a second pilgrimage to Mecca, but two months remained before the caravan would be ready to leave. Not wanting to waste the time, he journeyed to Mosul (in present Iraq) and Diyarbakir (in present Turkey). Near Mosul he saw wells of pitch such as he had heard about between Kufa and Basra. Tanks were constructed for it to collect in. The bitumen lay on the ground, deep black in color, glistening and soft. Ibn Battuta liked its odor. He reported:

Round the tanks is a large black pool, covered by a thin scum, which deposits on the edges. In the vicinity of this place there is a large spring, and when they wish to transport pitch from it, they light a fire over it, which dries up what watery moisture there is at that spot; then they cut it up into slabs and transport it.

Such was this early observer's recollection of what was to become one of the world's great oil regions.

While Ibn Battuta roamed in this remote land, he saw in the distance Mount Judi (about two hundred miles southwest of Mount Ararat), which the Koran mentioned as the place where Noah's ark came to rest. It impressed him as "lofty and high-soaring." He had already reverently viewed in Kufa an

37

open space beside a great mosque where Noah was said to have built his craft. Close by, a scholar had pointed out to the Moor the site of Noah's house and where the Koran said fountains of the deep had boiled up at the time of the flood. Thinking of that ancient man, Ibn Battuta breathed a blessing, "On him be peace."

He was back in Baghdad in time to take his place in the pilgrim caravan, where he had been assigned a camel litter, provisions, and water. His return to Mecca was uneventful, as he was ill with dysentery most of the way. On arrival he was so weak he had to go through the first day's ceremonies at the Kaaba seated. His sickness probably helped him reach a decision to remain in Mecca for a while. That year he returned to his Koranic studies and led what was for him a most agreeable existence. He'd had a sufficiency of travel for the time being and wanted to enjoy the scholarly surroundings.

He never said how he supported himself, but doubtless so personable an interpreter of Koranic law had no difficulty finding a place in the ecclesiastical community. He remained through 1328 and 1329 and then his itching foot bothered him again. The time had come for him to endeavor to visit India, where, he had been told, the emperor had brought together many servants from afar. Going there would involve a different way of travel for Ibn Battuta—he would make his first voyage by sea.

IV
To East Africa in a Dhow

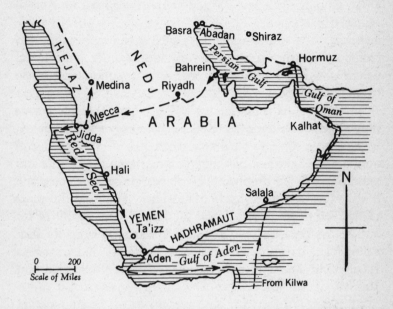

"No, thank you, I cannot bring myself to ride with the camels," Ibn Battuta told the kindly rich man who had invited him to sail to Yemen with him. Toward Yemen was the direction one took to reach India—that was the way Arab ships had been sailing for several hundred years.

Ibn Battuta was waiting to depart at Jidda, on Arabia's Red Sea coast, and the only kind of craft available were small wooden jalbas built of planks sewed together with coconut fiber and caulked with slivers of date palm. They were smeared over the outside with shark oil. Two rakish masts leaned over the open waist of each vessel to support triangular sails.

Although Ibn Battuta had lived by the ocean all of his early life, he had never before made a journey of any length over the water. His friend's boat was loaded with camels, and the Moor found the prospect of riding on the sea frightening enough without being stepped on by clumsy animals. He located another boat to take him on his way, but it was a poor affair, its only deck being at the poop, shaded with a roof of yellowed palm mats. The pilot steered with a yoke, beams, and ropes. The ship's master was naked to the waist, his shaggy hair bound with a scanty twist of cloth, a huge knife in his belt. Cooking on board was done in a sandbox, with rocks to support the pots.

At first it was monotonous sailing along the low, sandy brown coast bordering the Red Sea, but very shortly all that was changed. Banks of clouds gathered on a distant ridge of mountains, lightning flashing among them. Suddenly the wind faltered and dropped. The silence around the vessel was like a vault except for flocks of sea birds skimming the water in terrified flight. The sun was hidden, and only a bit of red and sullen sky was visible. The sea wakened from its dead calm, foam streaked the surface, a swell rose and drove the fragile craft ahead of it. The jalba pitched and rolled, and Ibn Battuta became seasick.

All that night the little boat was driven off its course, shipping water as waves broke over it. The Moor was not the only one of the passengers who was miserable. They all wanted to get off the vessel that seemed so likely to swamp and cast them into the water.

In the morning they were near a threatening headland on the African shore, surrounded with reefs. The sea was still rough, and Ibn Battuta feared the boat could not escape the pinnacles marking the entrance to a small bay inside the cape. He watched the pilot tug at his yoke with all his might. Several breathtaking moments passed, and then the boat was within the sheltered roadstead.

The Moor and the other passengers hastened ashore and took refuge in a hut shaped like a mosque. A party of black men armed with lances and swords approached, and the travelers persuaded them to rent camels for a land journey to the next port. Here a sturdier vessel was hired, bound for Yemen.

Even with a better boat, no sailing could be done at night because of the coral reefs spreading under the water like submerged tables. Each evening camp was made on shore, and everyone retired early because they had to be up again at sunrise and on their way.

It took six days sailing in this fashion to reach Hali, south of Jidda on the Arabian side of the Red Sea. This seems a complicated way in which to have covered the 250 miles in a direct line from Jidda, but travelers had little choice in that era. Ibn Battuta and his new friends brought their own supplies and lived on the hot deck, unsheltered from the dazzling sunlight except for the shade furnished by the triangular cotton sail.

There was nothing to do aboard the hot little ship but talk. The men shared their knowledge gathered by hearsay and in Ibn Battuta's case also from books. Five hundred years before, Arab captains had ventured far in their boats to China and the Sunda Islands (part of present Indonesia) to bring back spices. Some recorded the distances from place to place, telling of landmarks and leaving instructions for others to follow. In China they first saw the compass, which was more useful in making a landfall than sending up a shore-sighting bird. This had been the old custom of Indian merchants. They would free the bird, brought along for this purpose, and if it saw land on the horizon, it would fly in that direction, and they would follow. If not, it returned to the ship, and the sailors continued on. Arab navigators also learned to use the sun and stars to point the way. The Chinese, however, had their House of the Needle, or South-Pointing Chariot. The Arabs now carried such compasses—each consisting of a clay bowl of water in which floated a splinter of wood or straw carrying a magnetized needle.

41

Of course, nothing of the sort was needed on the Red Sea, where the water seemed to Ibn Battuta like a dull mirror, and the low shore was easily visible. Here it was the sudden winds and the numerous coral reefs that created the pilot's navigational problems.

At Hali it was several days before Ibn Battuta located another means of continuing his journey, this time accepting the invitation of the sultan to embark on one of his ships for a port in Yemen. Eventually the Moor reached the then capital of that country, Ta'izz, and accompanied a kadi to the sultan's audience. The ruler commanded the traveler to sit in front of him and asked questions about his country and about the monarchs of those he had passed through. As always, Ibn Battuta gave satisfactory answers and was rewarded with hospitable treatment and lodgings. The sultan sent him a horse, and on this he roamed to other cities in Yemen, finally reaching Aden, near the tip of the Arabian peninsula, where it was extremely hot.

Aden had neither trees nor fields, and all the water was from reservoirs that collected rain. All life in the town depended upon the monsoons. First there was the northeast wind that carried ships to Africa or across from India, which blew from December to March or April. The rest of the year the southwest wind blew the vessels home again.

The town was full of merchants, and trade was the great occupation. Around the edges of Aden's shallow bay Ibn Battuta saw dozens of small vessels propped on stilts or careened over on their sides while skirted sailors slapped hot whale grease on their hulls or pounded ragged coconut fiber into the seams. Gangs of sailmakers squatted on the sand, stitching with huge needles. Other men twisted coconut fiber from India into ship's cable.

Here and there Ibn Battuta watched carpenters scrape and gouge with adz and drill on the shapely curved bows of half-built dhows. These typically Arab vessels, with their high poops and twin lateen-rigged masts, have carried men and cargoes for centuries to and from Arab and East Indian ports. Though becoming scarcer, they can still be seen in this region today.

At the end of the stone jetty small craft discharged cargoes of dates and palm-leaf baskets. Out in the harbor the biggest dhows swung at anchor while longboats rowed back and forth to the rhythmic chant of sailors. The big ships stood with masts bare, waiting until their holds were full before their lateen sails would be hoisted.

Ibn Battuta soon learned he had chosen the wrong season for going to India. The ships were now getting ready for the annual voyage to Zanzibar and the Swahili lands down the East African coast. This opened another opportunity for Ibn Battuta to travel to strange places, so he changed his plan and boarded a dhow that was bound direct for the coast of present Somaliland.

The initial stop was at a dirty and disagreeable port that smelled so bad of fish and the blood of camels slaughtered in the street for meat that Ibn Battuta would not sleep ashore. For another fifteen days he sailed to Mogadiscio, a trading city founded by the Arabs several hundred years earlier. Many small high-prowed boats with lateen sails came out to meet the dhow, bringing young men laden with covered platters of food. It was their custom each to claim a merchant, take him home, and sell his goods.

"This man is not a merchant," the seamen said when one of the fellows approached Ibn Battuta. "He is a doctor of law."

"This is then the guest of the kadi," the townsman exclaimed. But the traveler found it was not to be so. The kadi sent a student to tell him he must first see the sultan before taking lodging.

"Our master commands that you be lodged in the students' house" was the next order.

The kadi led the Moor there, and a boy arrived bringing large wooden platters from the palace. In them were rice cooked with butter, meats, chicken, fish, vegetables, cooked bananas, pickled lemons, pickled peppers, green ginger, and mangoes.

Ibn Battuta noticed that the men of Mogadiscio ate very large helpings, and he supposed this was why they were extremely fat. The conserves were highly seasoned, and their meals must have been much like East Indian curries. He learned about other unaccustomed ways when the vizier (a high councillor of state) brought him a set of robes to wear to the mosque service when he would see the sultan.

The visitor was expected to divest himself of his regular garments and put on those of the country. To his dismay he discovered he was not supposed to wear drawers.

"They have no acquaintance with these," he was told.

Instead he must tie a silk cloth around his waist. Above this went an embroidered linen tunic, a furred mantle and a turban with an embroidered edge. He put these on and joined the kadi at the mosque. After prayers the sultan welcomed Ibn Battuta, then a procession formed and followed the ruler to his palace on foot. The sultan walked under silk canopies surmounted with golden birds. Musicians with drums, trumpets, and fifes went ahead of him. Ibn Battuta was permitted to sit in the audience room a long, tedious time as a respected guest, but actually nothing interesting happened.

The dhow was ready to sail again, and the next stop was at Mombasa (a seaport in present Kenya) for one night. For all his weeks at sea off the East African coast, Ibn Battuta did not see much country. The end of the vessel's run was at Kilwa (in present Tanzania), a big city of wooden buildings roofed with reeds. Here he made the acquaintance of another sultan, noted for his generosity.

The Moor had now been halfway down the East African coast, but was unable to absorb much knowledge about it.

During his stay in Kilwa the dhow was careened, and her hull was scraped and oiled. She was loaded deep with mangrove wood and ivory, and about the end of March, when the season of the southwest monsoon set in, she was ready to sail north at a fast clip.

This time the destination was the coast of Hadhramaut on the south side of the Arabian peninsula facing the Gulf of Aden and the Arabian Sea. Once more Ibn Battuta was in his element, observing how men lived. He noted that little fish resembling sardines were being caught to feed livestock, and he saw vines that produced betel leaves for chewing. Most remarkable to him were the coconut palms bearing what he called "Indian nuts."

He wrote:

The nut resembles a man's head, for it has marks like eyes and a mouth and the contents, when it is green, are like the brain. It has fibre like hair, out of which they make ropes, which they use instead of nails to bind their ships together and also as cables. Among its properties are that it strengthens the body, fattens and adds redness to the face. If it is cut open when it is green it gives a liquid deliciously sweet and fresh. After drinking this one takes a piece of the rind as a spoon and scrapes out the pulp. This tastes like an egg that has been broiled but not quite cooked and is nourishing.

He was not yet through with relating the marvels of the coconut.

One of its peculiarities is that oil, milk and honey are extracted from it. The honey is made by cutting a stalk on which the fruit grows, leaving two fingers' length, and on this they tie a small bowl into which the sap drips. If this has been done in the morning, a servant climbs up again in the evening with two bowls, one filled with water. He pours into the

45

*other the collected sap, then washes the stalk, cuts off a piece
and ties on another bowl. The same thing is repeated next
morning until a good deal has been collected, when the sap
is cooked until it thickens. It then makes an excellent honey
and the merchants of India, Yemen and China buy it and
take it to their own countries, where they manufacture sweetmeats from it.*

*To make oil the ripe nuts are peeled and the contents dried
in the sun, then cooked in cauldrons and the oil extracted.
They use it for lighting and dip bread in it and the women
put it on their hair.*

After leaving the Hadhramaut coast in a little vessel bound
for the Gulf of Oman (near the mouth of the Persian Gulf),
Ibn Battuta stopped at an island where he observed another
unusual sight, the gathering of the spicy-scented gum of the
frankincense bush. This was one of the world's most precious
perfumes, and men had gone to Arabia to fetch it since ancient times.

Ibn Battuta noted that the people on this island lived in
houses made of fish bones with camel skins for roofs. What he
saw must have been whale bones.

This voyage along the eastern extremity of the Arabian
peninsula was extremely trying. A violent storm blew up, and
a merchant vessel in sight ahead of Ibn Battuta's boat sank.
All on board her drowned except one man who managed to
swim long enough to be rescued. Another unpleasantness was
due to the Moor's dislike of the way the sailors gathered sea
birds for food and failed to kill them in the orthodox Muslim
manner, which was by slitting their throats. On this account
Ibn Battuta did not want to eat them, so he got along on
dried dates and broiled bits of fish.

In due course the little vessel rounded the cape at the
mouth of the Gulf of Oman and anchored at noon in front
of a seashore village. On a slope thirteen miles away Ibn

Battuta could see the city of Kalhat. He wanted to get away from the boat, so he and a fellow passenger hired one of the sailors to guide them to the large town. They did not know they had made a poor choice of cicerone and that the seaman was out to rob them.

The traveler left most of his possessions on board with the rest of his party, who were to join him next day, but he gave a bundle of clothing to the man to carry. As a precaution against attack, Ibn Battuta brought along a lance.

The guide led the two travelers along shore to an inlet and, wading into it, indicated that they could cross there.

Ibn Battuta became suspicious and ordered, "You cross alone and leave the clothes. We will watch, and if you succeed we shall follow you, otherwise we will look for a ford higher up."

The man drew back, and his plot became clear when they saw people swimming farther out in the inlet. This confirmed Ibn Battuta's guess that the water was too deep. He was certain that the guide wished to drown his charges and make away with the bundle of clothes. The Moor was alarmed at what might happen in this isolated spot. He brandished his lance and indicated they would go the long way around, which meant crossing a dry plain.

Ibn Battuta and his friend had been out a good many hours and were extremely thirsty, until a lone horseman came along and offered them drinks from his waterskin. Kalhat looked close at hand, but they discovered gullies separated them from the town, and there were miles yet to go. The tricky guide was still trying to mislead them, evidently hoping to get the pair off in a lonely place where he would be able to rob them.

Night was coming on, and they were nowhere near the town. It was soon too dark to see the way, and they were so weary from traversing the gullies that they would have to stop and rest. Besides, there might be other evil-intentioned persons abroad.

"The right course is to turn off the track and sleep," Ibn Battuta told his companion.

The man wanted to go on, as he was again very thirsty.

"No, it is preferable to go into hiding," insisted the Moor. He admitted to himself that he was completely exhausted.

Selecting a spot by a tree where they could sleep on the ground, he put the guide in the middle in order to watch him. Ibn Battuta lay down on top of his bundle and grasped his lance. He dared not sleep. Every time the guide moved the Moor spoke to him so that he would know he was under surveillance.

It was a long and fearful night for Ibn Battuta, but he got through it, and in the morning the situation improved. On the path again, they met persons going to town with produce and were able to obtain water to drink. There were still ravines and ridges to cross. The Moor's feet had swelled in his soft shoes, and he was afraid his toes would begin to bleed under the nails.

Eventually the travelers reached Kalhat exhausted, only to have the town gatekeeper put a finishing touch to their misery. "You must go with me to the governor," he insisted, "that he may be informed of what you are doing and where you have come from."

Fortunately the governor proved to be a compassionate man and understood their distress. He invited Ibn Battuta to remain as his guest. It was six days before the latter could walk again with comfort.

He was not far from the Persian port of Hormuz (near present Bandar Abbas), where there was a possibility of finding a ship bound for India, since that city was a large trading center for goods from the East. Again Ibn Battuta had arrived at the wrong season, so he decided to continue his travels by land, rather than lose time waiting for the winds to change. He stayed in Hormuz more than two weeks and remarked upon an unusual sight, a whale's head set in the gate of the principal mosque.

"The eyes were like doors," he recalled, "and you would see people entering by one eye and coming out the other."

The vizier, who had received him with the customary hospitality, upon being reminded that Ibn Battuta would like to meet the sultan, took the Moor's hand and accompanied him to the palace. There they encountered an old man in untidy garments and wearing a kerchief as girdle. The vizier saluted him, so Ibn Battuta did the same, but then turned and began conversing with a young man he had met, who was the sultan's nephew.

Ibn Battuta did not know he had just snubbed the ruler. The dirty old man was none other than the sultan. When the vizier so informed him, Ibn Battuta was covered with confusion. There were times when he didn't always do the right thing.

The sultan got up and went inside to his audience room, so they followed the notables in. There was the sultan sitting on his throne in the same shabby garments, but fingering a rosary made of magnificent pearls. This time he asked Ibn Battuta about himself and his journey and the rulers he had met.

The audience was brief, as the sultan had his mind on a war he was waging against his relatives who had fled to islands in the Persian Gulf, where the rich pearl fisheries were.

Traveling in the country beyond Hormuz, Ibn Battuta was told, was dangerous, so he hired mounts of local tribesmen and joined their caravan. Because of the great heat they slept by day and rode by night. In this way he reached the gulf near the pearl fisheries.

Ibn Battuta did not have a clear idea about the real nature of pearls. He saw that divers wore masks of tortoise shells clipped to the nose and went down on a rope, gathering the oyster shells from the bottom and putting them in a leather bag slung around the neck. But like many other Arabs of that day, he understood that when the oysters were brought up and came in contact with the air, their flesh solidified and turned into gems. This was not true. The pearls were made of a hard shining substance called nacre, which the oysters secreted around irritating grains of sand or other minute objects which had gotten inside the shells.

Ibn Battuta next crossed to Bahrein (a city then on the mainland, not on today's island in the Persian Gulf). He rambled around in that vicinity, then turned into the desert in the direction of the modern city of Riyadh. He was in time to join the caravan of an emir who was about to make the pilgrimage of 1332 to Mecca. So back Ibn Battuta went to the holy city, joyful that he could do so.

He experienced true religious zeal every time he went there. Ibn Battuta explained it in his own words: "Allah has printed in the heart of men the desire to come to the holy shrine for this reunion of Believers. He has inspired an all-powerful love; no one comes here but Allah takes possession of his heart."

At the conclusion of this, his fourth pilgrimage season, Ibn Battuta went down to Jidda again to cross the Red Sea. He had not been able to get to India by the customary means, but maybe that was God's will. Had not the dream in Fuwa foretold that he should go there by way of the land of the Turks?

Well, that was what he would now endeavor to do.

V

The Romantic Land of Rum

Once more Ibn Battuta was preparing to board a vessel, but the experience would be very different from cruising in Arab dhows. He would be among barbarians, men who did not understand Arabic. It required courage and tact to plunge into another world where customs and language were unknown to him.

Until now the Moor had journeyed on routes frequented by pilgrims, and they were respected. Although the spoken dialects of scattered countries might be hard for him to understand, wherever he found educated persons, the written language had always been the same, for the Koran was the basis of all Islamic learning.

Ibn Battuta had again crossed the Red Sea from Jidda to the Egyptian side, hired camels and black guides and traversed the desert to the Nile Valley. With a fellow pilgrim he joined another party traveling on horseback through Syria to the port of Latakia, where ships left for the land of Rum.

In those days Asia Minor (present Anatolia or Asiatic Turkey) was called by this old name, given it for the Romans who had conquered the country early in the Christian era. Later Turkish nomadic invaders came out of Asia and in the eleventh century set up small kingdoms ruled by dynasties known as the Seljuk sultans, for one of their ancestors who was supposed to have lived to the age of 107. More than a century before Ibn Battuta's journey, another invasion, that of the Mongols, toppled the Seljuk regime and left Rum fragmented into tiny kingdoms. The Turks, however, still ruled these independent little sultanates. They had brought the Islamic religion and spread it over the scattered Roman and Greek provinces, but their teaching was in another language. (Turkish is the only language into which the Koran was officially permitted to be translated, though today it is printed in about forty tongues. The object was to keep the word of God unadulterated.)

Ibn Battuta knew that once he got into Rum, which was after all a Muslim land, he might expect to encounter the custom of giving hospitality and alms to travelers. But from Latakia to the Seljuk port of Alanya (in present Turkey, some miles from the larger port of Antalya), he must sail in an infidel galley. He was directed to a large one captained by a Genoese. Instead of the rope-sewn planks, triangular sails, and fish-oil coatings of the Arab vessels, it was brightly painted blue and red, with the round high stern and prow gilded. Its mast was thick, with a round platform for the lookout on top. The sail was square and striped gaily yellow and blue. There was a deep hold for cargo and banks of oars. On the high gilded afterdeck were cabins and the captain's quarters with a bed, armchairs, a table, an hourglass, an astrolabe, and such crude charts of the coast as existed.

These surroundings and comforts at sea surprised the Moor, as also did the captain's hospitality. He refused payment for the voyage. The trip lasted ten nights and days, a long time for a relatively short distance, but with only oars and weak winds for power, this is understandable. The ship crossed the Gulf of Alexandretta (present Iskenderon Gulf), with the coastline in sight most of the time. Sailing in the placid Mediterranean was a restful interlude, lacking the extreme heat and the sudden winds of the African coast.

Ibn Battuta's destination was a beautiful harbor, once the principal port of the Seljuk kings. A tall octagonal red-stone castle dominated the waterfront fortifications. To the south of it were five brick-lined vaulted galleries of the naval base, each high enough to shelter a ship. Flat-roofed houses of the town rose along the slope of a hill among scattered trees, and above them walls climbed to a citadel on the summit.

The Moor parted with the friendly shipmaster and went ashore in this truly alien land. He observed at once that its inhabitants were lighter of skin than in the desert countries, and the women were not veiled. Many foreign merchants lodged in separate quarters in the town, and there was a mixture of languages. Ibn Battuta, desiring to find someone who knew Arabic, sought out the kadi.

Profiting from past experience, he told the judge, "I wish to meet your ruler."

The ruler did not live in the citadel but out in the country ten miles away. The kadi took the visitor there and acted as interpreter when the ruler asked many questions. He was kindly and gave the Moor a parting gift of money for the road.

Having made this good a start, Ibn Battuta and his companions arranged for horses to carry them west along the coast to Antalya, another walled city. They found it surrounded by apricot orchards. The fruit was ripe at this season and was much to the Moor's liking. He had heard of a college where there lived a sheikh who understood Arabic, so he asked the way to it and was given lodging there.

Next day a cobbler in shabby clothes and felt cap called at the sheikh's house and invited Ibn Battuta to bring his companions to dine that night.

"This is a poor fellow," the Moor said to the sheikh, "and I do not wish to incommode him. What shall I do?"

The sheikh laughed and assured him, "The cobbler is a man of generous disposition, and he has about two hundred associates from different trades. They elected him their leader and built a hospice in which to entertain guests. All they earn by day they spend by night. By all means go and visit them."

The cobbler arrived after evening prayer and escorted Ibn Battuta and his friends to an attractive building furnished inside with beautiful carpets, luster glass, divans around the walls, and five huge brass candelabra. Standing about the large main room were young men in long cloaks, boots, and peaked white headdresses from each of which hung a felt tube. All carried a long knife in their wide girdles.

When the guests were led to a platform and seated, the feast was brought in. The young men removed their headdresses and replaced them with silk scarves before sitting down to eat.

Ibn Battuta was astonished at the whole scene. He did not know he was to find these guilds of young men everywhere he went in the land of Rum. There was nothing like them in any other nation. True, the Moor had visited hospices elsewhere, but in none was there evidence of such an intense desire to please strangers, serve them foods, supply their wants, and share with them an intimate sort of sociability.

It was the custom in Asia Minor for these hospices to be furnished comfortably and elegantly with rugs and lamps. Men of the brotherhoods worked at their trades in daytime and following afternoon prayer brought their collective earnings to their leader so that he might spend the money for their communal needs. If a stranger arrived in town, the brotherhood entertained him. After eating, the men danced and sang, circling to the music of reed flutes.

The Moor was not accustomed to Muslim believers who indulged in music, but the whole performance seemed very well intentioned, and he decided he must accustom himself to such sights in foreign countries. (The mysterious brotherhoods Ibn Battuta found and was the first person to describe are known to historians as orders of dervishes.) The young men appeared of noble disposition, exceedingly generous, and they said good night to their guests with great cordiality. Ibn Battuta supposed they were an exception to the rule, but at the very next town he reached, a group of young men came out and invited the travelers to spend the night with them. Ibn Battuta, still not altogether trustful, made other arrangements, nevertheless he could not refuse a banquet they offered him in a garden. No matter that they could not understand each other's language and had no one to interpret, they still seemed happy to entertain him.

He soon memorized the Turkish words by which he could ask the way to the judge, the sheikh, or the seminary, and thus he was able to find some person who might interpret for him. In small villages there usually was no one, but for the most part people were disposed to be friendly. He encountered stretches of road with few persons in sight and others with much foot travel and occasional horsemen.

Word of the arrival of a distinguished-looking young stranger and his party spread quickly in those remote settlements, and Ibn Battuta was more welcome than a wandering troubadour, representing as he did a fresh contact with the outside world.

It was the month of May in the year 1331, and the season of Ramadan began. The travelers reached Egridir in time for the evening breaking of the fast, and the sultan of this small kingdom invited them to join him in the ceremony.

55

They went to his romantic-looking walled castle, and he shared with his guests a great bowl of crumbled bread topped with lentils soaked in butter and sugar. Then other platters of food were brought in, and they enjoyed a magnificent feast. At parting, the sultan sent along with Ibn Battuta a handsome horse, rich clothing, and money.

Ibn Battuta accepted these as a just reward. He exerted himself to be entertaining when his hosts questioned him about other lands and the knowledge he had gleaned in Mecca. As long as someone present could interpret for him, he was in his element, an Arab forerunner of the visiting professor and traveling lecturer. His personality and charm earned him gifts from all the sultans along the way, so that up to now he had no problems.

But all of Rum was not filled with hospitable cities. There were great stretches of open country infested with brigands, where the scattered towns were heavily fortified. At one place when his party joined a caravan, they reached a great walled castle at night and were not permitted to enter. They made camp in the desolate country outside it, and next morning inhabitants called down from the top of the wall asking why they were there and whence they had come.

Before he was satisfied of the travelers' peaceful intentions, the commander of the castle sallied forth at the head of a file of troops to make certain no robbers were in their midst or were concealed anywhere nearby. Then the caravan was permitted to enter.

The route inside another one of these walled cities led through a bazaar. Suddenly, as the Moor passed, men leaped out from the stalls and seized the bridles of the horses. Before Ibn Battuta could think of a way out of his predicament another group approached, shouting protests at the merchants who had detained him. A bitter quarrel broke out, knives were unsheathed, and the Moor was convinced he was to be the victim of the bandits about whom he had heard so much. No one in his party could understand the shouts of the combatants, and it appeared that the fight was over who should rob the new arrivals.

Out of the melee rose a voice and a familiar greeting in Arabic. "I am a pilgrim," the man identified himself. "I can speak for you."

"What do they want of us?" the Moor asked.

"Have no fear," laughed the man. "They are members of two brotherhoods. Both want you to lodge with them."

Ibn Battuta found it extraordinary that men should do battle for a chance to show hospitality. He couldn't quite accustom himself to the strange ways of these brotherhoods. The two factions resolved their controversy by casting lots in the market street. It was decided the travelers would go first to one group and then afterward to the second group.

Undaunted by finding few persons who could speak the language of the Prophet, the Moor journeyed pleasantly for many weeks across the plateau and into eastern Turkey as far as Erzincan and Erzurum, being hospitably received everywhere and accumulating knowledge of the country. No other person has left a record of what it was like there in the century before the Ottoman Empire rose to power.

Back he journeyed once more to western Turkey, where the coastal valleys run down to the Aegean Sea. At Birgi, near present Aydin, Ibn Battuta met a wealthy professor who insisted on sending him into the hills to meet the sultan, who had gone to a summer camp in a walnut grove to escape the heat. Although the professor was suffering from a boil on his foot, he would not think of having the eminent traveler left without an interpreter. The savant wrapped his sore foot carefully so that it would not come in contact with the stirrup and made the trip to the royal camp in the highlands.

Here for the first time Ibn Battuta was lodged in a curious felt tent shaped over laths in the form of a cupola. The upper part could be opened for ventilation. The Moor learned that this was a type of habitation the Turkomans had brought from their Asiatic homeland.

The sultan was exceedingly pleased that Ibn Battuta had gone out of his way for this visit to his summer court. He asked about places where the Moor had been, invited him to meals, and requested the learned guest to write down a number of the sayings of the Prophet for him. The professor was commanded to translate these into Turkish.

So enraptured was the sultan with his visitor that he delayed Ibn Battuta's departure several days. The traveler, restless to be on his way again, asked leave to continue his journey, whereupon a court officer appeared and asked what gifts he would care to receive.

"The sultan has at his disposal gold and silver, horses and slaves. Let him give whatever he likes," the professor suggested.

The deputy returned shortly, saying, "The sultan commands you both to remain here today and go down with him tomorrow to his residence in the city."

There was no choice but to wait again. When the royal party arrived in Birgi, the population came out to greet them. Ibn Battuta rode along calmly on a beautiful horse to the palace gate, wondering what was in store for him. Within the vestibule of the palace, twenty pale handsome youths in silken robes awaited the ruler.

"Who are they?" Ibn Battuta asked the professor.

"They are Greek pages" was the reply.

The visitors accompanied the sultan up a long flight of stone stairs to an audience hall which had an ornamental pool in its center and a bronze lion at each corner. The lions spouted water from their mouths. Around the hall were benches covered with rugs, a special one having the sultan's great cushion.

All sat down, and servants brought gold and silver bowls of fruit syrup in which pieces of biscuit floated. There were gold and silver spoons for eating this sweet. At the same time the servants brought pottery bowls and wooden spoons, in case anyone had Muslim scruples about eating with precious utensils.

The sultan asked Ibn Battuta, "Have you ever seen a stone that fell from the sky?"

"I have never seen one, nor ever heard tell of one," the Moor replied.

"Well," the sultan continued, "a stone did fall from the sky outside this town of ours." He commanded some men to bring it in.

The rock was large, black, hard, glittering, and very heavy. The sultan ordered stonebreakers to beat on it with hammers, but they made no impression.

Ibn Battuta was confounded. It was the only time he ever examined a meteorite, and he did not know how to explain it. (He may already have seen one other, for the black stone at the Kaaba in Mecca could have had such an origin.)

Getting away from Birgi was a long-delayed process. Two days later the sultan gave a banquet to which he invited all the notables from round about. Ibn Battuta lodged at the college, where every night the sultan sent him food, fruit, sweetmeats, and candles. Finally came a large sum of gold, a complete set of garments, and a gift of one of the handsome youths, a Greek slave named Michael. (In those days, everyone who could afford it owned slaves as servants, and many Greeks, captured by Turks in their wars against Byzantium, had been enslaved.) To each of the Moor's companions also went a robe and some coins.

What with the stay on the mountain and the stay in town, two weeks passed before Ibn Battuta got on the road to Aya Saluk, the Turkish name for ancient Ephesus. Here was located one of the world's most magnificent mosques, formerly the Greek church of St. John. Its walls were of colored marbles and the paving of white marble, while the lead roof supported eleven domes of different sizes.

The Moor also went to see another church made of great

stones. It had been erected on the foundations of the famous Temple of Diana. Without knowing it, Ibn Battuta was looking at the site of yet another Wonder of the Ancient World. He had already seen the Pharos of Alexandria and the Great Pyramid of Egypt; now he was attending Friday service at a place where the Greeks had erected a magnificent temple. The Moor was not impressed by the ancient stones, for being a pious Muslim he was more interested in the works of God than in those of man.

A few days later Michael and the slave of one of Ibn Battuta's companions took the horses to water and failed to return. The Moor was ready to depart, and he waited impatiently and had unflattering thoughts about the dependability of Greek slaves. He was angry at the delay and frustrated because he had no way of inquiring about the missing pair, who he was sure had run away. He had been too willing to trust them. Determined to find his horses, he sought an Arabic-speaking professor and prevailed on the scholar to accompany him to the local sultan to report the theft.

It was not until the next afternoon that the fugitives were found. Some Turks, seeing them on the road, became suspicious that lads, unaccompanied, should be riding such fine mounts. They stopped Michael and forced a confession out of him. Thus Ibn Battuta got his horses and slave back, feeling he had learned a lesson about placing too much reliance on the honesty of fellow travelers.

Not long afterward the party made camp with a group of Turkomans who were pasturing horses. Ibn Battuta decided it would be very easy for them to rob him, so he and his companions took turns standing guard. When it was time for the Moor to be sentry, he kept awake by reciting passages from the Koran. Nevertheless, when the mounts were brought in, one of the horses purchased in Aya Saluk, along with its bridle and saddle, was missing. The horse herders had departed early, and there was no recourse.

The travelers were approaching the Sea of Marmara, and they hired a man to guide them over steep and rugged mountains to Balikesir. In this town Ibn Battuta bought a pretty Greek slave girl, Margherita. Under what circumstances he did so never was told, but the Moor must have tired of having no woman companion for he was twenty-seven years old. He had taken a Muslim wife once on the road to Damascus, but they had parted there, the bride remaining with her own family.

The Moor was now very close to Constantinople (present Istanbul), the renowned capital of the Byzantine Empire, about which he had been hearing for a long time. There was no chance of visiting it from Turkey, as the two nations constantly made war upon each other. Bursa, which Ibn Battuta next entered, had been conquered in 1326 from the Greeks of Byzantium, and in the brief time since had become the capital of the Ottoman sultans. Orkhan was the second of this line of Turkish rulers, and he was one monarch the Moor was unable to approach. Whatever regrets Ibn Battuta had were offset to some extent when he continued on his way northeast and arrived at Iznik. Orkhan's sultana was living there, and she received the traveler and sent him lavish gifts.

Ibn Battuta's party was much reduced in numbers, and he hesitated to set out on winter treks through mountainous country. His best horse was sick, and he waited far into November for it to recover, then gave up and had to leave it behind. When he again took the road, he had Margherita, the two slave boys, and only three other companions—a small group to be traveling unescorted in such a forbidding land. A man who had served as interpreter left at Iznik, and there was no person to replace him. Ibn Battuta had no choice but to continue and trust to finding his way despite the wintry weather and the obstacles ahead.

The first night's stop was thirty miles east of Iznik. In the morning the party followed a Turkish woman who was on a horse, accompanied by a servant, and bound for the next town. They arrived at the Sakarya River, and the woman went ahead to ford it. Ibn Battuta's group reached the bank just as her horse went down in the stream and threw the woman into the water. Her servant jumped in after her, but the swift-flowing river carried both away. Ibn Battuta watched men on the opposite bank swim out and bring the woman in, too late to save her life.

The tragedy caused the Moor to halt and consider what he should do. Persons who had gathered on the bank gestured that this was no place to cross the Sakarya and indicated that the better spot was downstream. Ibn Battuta followed the direction in which they pointed and came to a curious ferry consisting of four sections of wood tied together with ropes. The owner indicated the travelers were to pile saddles and baggage on this crude raft, then get on it themselves. They were pulled to the opposite side while the horses were led across swimming.

This eastern country near the Black Sea was more primitive than the western coast of Rum, and persons familiar with Arabic were harder to find than ever. At one hospice the members of the brotherhood summoned a lawyer to act as interpreter, but it turned out that he spoke Persian, not Arabic. He pompously excused himself, claiming, "These visitors speak ancient Arabic. I know new Arabic."

At another stopping place the travelers lodged in the house of an old woman who was not a Muslim. Nothing grew at the place except saffron, and the woman, thinking they were merchants, brought out her product to sell, but found no buyers. That night there was a heavy snowfall, which obliterated the road.

A horseman whom the brotherhood had sent to guide the party went ahead and picked his way to a Turkoman village, which they reached at midday. Here the guide had to turn back, but he arranged for a Turkoman to ride on with his charges. This was menacing country, all woods, mountains, and gullies, a poor place for an Arab from desert lands to be in cold weather. Ibn Battuta was thankful for the warm garments he had been given since coming to Rum.

For a while the travelers followed a stream, crossing it more than thirty times, then they arrived at an especially desolate spot where the Turkish guide stopped and delivered an ultimatum:

"Give me some money!"

"When we reach the next town, we shall give you all you want," Ibn Battuta told him. He had learned some words of Turkish in recent months, but the man may not have understood.

He persisted in holding out his hand belligerently.

Reluctantly Ibn Battuta gave him several coins, and the fellow immediately disappeared in the direction from which they had come.

There was no one left in the party who had the least idea which way to go, snow having hidden all traces of trails and roads. Trying to guess where the route went, the travelers kept on. Finally at sunset they reached a hill where the track was indicated by a quantity of stones.

It was nearly dark, and Ibn Battuta feared he and his companions would perish out there in the snow. The sky was threatening, and probably more of the white stuff would come down in the night. He did not think Allah intended him to die in this lonely spot when he had already survived so many other difficulties.

"I have a good horse, a thoroughbred," he told himself. "If I go on and reach safety, I may contrive some means to save my companions."

He arranged a shelter for them out of the saddles and saddlebags propped against the stones. Commending his companions to God, he set out in the dark night through the trackless snow. After a time he saw in the distance a cluster of little wooden structures, which he thought might be coops for poultry or small animals. Instead, when he came up to them, they proved to be burial places. Where there was death, there must also be life, he reasoned, blundering on through the cemetery and the wilderness beyond. Well after the hour of night prayer, he discerned the dim shapes of real houses. They appeared so dark he feared they might be empty, but as he said later, God guided him to a building where there was an old man. Ibn Battuta saluted him, asking if he understood Arabic. The fellow replied in Turkish, signaling him to enter.

Ibn Battuta saw with relief that he was in another hospice of the brothers. He endeavored to describe the plight of his companions far back on the trail. One of the men inside understood him—he had encountered the Moor previously on the road and knew about the little party of strangers.

The brethren went at once to the rescue, the Moor accompanying them. With great relief he found his company unharmed and huddling close together for warmth under their coverlets in the snow. Inhabitants of a village beyond the hospice brought what food they could spare, and the party was well cared for the rest of the night.

At dawn they rode on again to a town west of present Bolu, where they found the hospice full of travelers and no stable available. It was Friday, and they went to the mosque, anxious as to how to proceed because of the snow and the cold. There they encountered a Turk who had made the Hajj to Mecca and was able to greet them in Arabic.

"Where can we stable our horses? It is very cold for them," Ibn Battuta inquired.

"One cannot manage to tether the animals inside any building here," the man said, "because the doors are too small for horses to get through, but I shall take you to a covered arcade in the bazaar, where travelers tie their mounts."

He guided them to this place, and one of the companions settled in an empty shop alongside to guard the animals. A servant went to buy hay to feed them.

Weary of his language difficulties in this alien territory, Ibn Battuta requested the pilgrim to accompany his party as far as the city of Kastamonu, which was said to be another ten days' journey distant. (Today all these places in northeastern Turkey are only a few hours apart by automobile road.) He gave the man expense money and an Egyptian robe and assigned him a spare horse to ride, promising him a good reward when they reached their destination. It soon became evident that the new member of the party was out to cheat the others when he made purchases of food in the bazaars. His thefts became so outrageous Ibn Battuta would say each evening, "Well, Haji, how much expense money have you stolen today?"

The man would reply, "Oh, so much," and everyone would laugh and make the best of it because, lacking Turkish, they did not know what else to do.

One night they lodged in a certain village at the house of the fellow's sister. She brought stewed dried fruits and other treats, and when Ibn Battuta went to pay her, the pilgrim said, "Don't give her anything—give it to me."

Ibn Battuta secretly paid the sister, vowing to separate himself from this miser as soon as possible.

Another day the travelers reached a small, swift river, and the Moor sent the boys across to see how safe it was to ford. They made it without difficulty, so the companions followed, stripping off their heavy outer garments and tying them in bundles on the saddles. One led Margherita's horse, but as the swirling water deepened around her, she became dizzy.

"Wait, I will take you behind me on my saddle," Ibn Battuta offered. He drew her gently on behind him, and they started out again. Midway in the river the horse stumbled on the rocks. Margherita fell off while Ibn Battuta struggled to swim the animal in the turbulent water. He shouted, and the boys plunged into the river at once, but by the time they had pulled the girl out she was drowned.

Wet, cold, and dismayed, they gathered on the bank. It

65

was a repetition of the sad sight they had witnessed at the Sakarya. One moment Margherita had been with them, the next moment she was gone. They were all shocked, for the Greek maid had won a place in their hearts. Scarce knowing what he was doing, Ibn Battuta made arrangements to bury her. There was nothing else, no other service he could perform, and with a great sense of loss, he mounted his horse and went on.

Chilled to the skin, the travelers continued to the next town, where fortunately they found a hospice of the brethren. It was a welcome sight to see fireplaces in the corners of the main room and be able to warm themselves and dry out. Still oppressed by sadness, Ibn Battuta removed his wet clothing, toasted himself at the fire, and was fed. He would always remember the Turkish hearths and chimneys, like nothing he had ever encountered elsewhere. Again he praised the unselfish brotherhood for their compassion to strangers.

The party went the rest of the way to Kastamonu without difficulty, and finding living cheap there, they remained forty days, recovering from their travels. They purchased their own firewood and supplies, and Ibn Battuta told later of bargains they found in fat mutton, honey sweetmeats, walnuts, and chestnuts. (They were in the midst of nut-growing country.)

In this town lived several learned men who spoke Arabic and had been to Mecca. The sultan, stately and venerable and past seventy years of age, gave the Moor an audience, provided lodging and sent gifts of a thoroughbred horse, a robe, and money. He also assigned some of the harvest of wheat and barley from a nearby village to Ibn Battuta, but it had so little value in this city of cheap prices that the traveler gave away what his people could not use.

With his animals rested and his energy renewed, the Moor continued by a main road down to the Black Sea and the fortified city of Sinop. The place was governed by the son of the sultan of Kastamonu, so Ibn Battuta had no difficulty in gaining permission to enter.

He was now nearly at the end of his wanderings in the land of Rum and ready to penetrate another completely unknown realm lying far across the stormy waters. The gray-stone turrets of Sinop looked upon a harbor filled with Greek galleys and Genoese carracks, but departure from this port was not to be quickly accomplished. Few captains would venture upon the Black Sea in winter, and the Moor waited a month and a half in a hospice before he found a galley that would take him to the city of Kiram (present Stary Krjm) in the Crimea.

It was early spring, and the first pink flush was on the Judas trees when he joined several merchants who had engaged the vessel, and they sailed out of Sinop. Before leaving he freed his slaves. The dark, wooded shores of Asia Minor faded from sight, and after a few hours the southwest wind filled the large lateen sail, and the narrow ship turned her long sharp prow out across the seemingly boundless sea.

For three days the galley moved on to the measured splash of long oars when the wind slackened. Ibn Battuta had time to reflect upon his experiences in the country where he had spent the past year, where he had gained a wealth of gifts from generous rulers, and where he had briefly lavished affection on the young Greek girl.

What lay ahead in the vast reaches of the East? The Arab geographers had told little about it, and he had encountered no travelers who had followed this circuitous route to India.

Ibn Battuta's reflections were interrupted when the weather turned gusty, a gale came shrieking off the Russian steppes, and the frail galley was driven back toward the coast of Rum. Waves rolled high, breaking over the bulwarks, pouring across the deck and running off in torrents. This was more terrible than the storm on the Red Sea. The ship shuddered and groaned ominously for hours on end.

A man from Maghrib, Ibn Battuta's own country, shared a cabin in the stern with him, and just before the hour of night prayer, he went on deck to see if there was any sign of the weather moderating. As the Moor was spreading his prayer rug, the fellow rushed back, crying excitedly, "I commend you to God. In a matter of a few minutes we shall sink!"

Ibn Battuta touched his forehead to the prayer mat and murmured, "Allah help us."

He feared his hour had come, that his wanderings were to end in these stormy waters far from his native land.

VI

Rolling Tents on the Russian Steppes

Although driven back nearly to Sinop, the galley did not sink. But Ibn Battuta could not get off it soon enough. He had had all he wanted of travel on this inland ocean. It was a sea that geographers had mentioned in telling of the great silk route from China. Since the eighth century Arabs had told of crossing the Black Sea to get to the mouth of the Don River and to reach the Caspian Sea to trade, but these venturesome merchants were few and far between. Black Sea ports had long been the province of Greek traders. Genoese and Venetian galleys also came this way, and Marco Polo had traveled to the port of Trabzon and gone over the mountains from there to Tabriz and Hormuz, both places Ibn Battuta already had visited.

Since he had vowed never to retrace his steps if possible,

he was following a more roundabout and complicated route. He knew that he would find Muslims among the Tatars and Mongols on the north shore of the sea. He had heard others tell of their lands when he passed through Iran and Turkey, but there was no reliable information to prepare him for their customs, only wonder tales passed on from person to person.

The country he now looked upon was verdant but treeless, yet it was more inviting than tossing about in the galley any longer.

"I wish to descend anywhere here," he told the captain.

Some of the merchants were of similar persuasion, so the shipmaster put them ashore where a church dominated a tiny village. The group made for this building as a temporary place of refuge. Its sole occupant was a monk.

Ibn Battuta observed that on one of the walls inside was the painted figure of a man who seemed to be an Arab wearing a turban. A sword was in his belt and a spear in one hand, and in front of him was a lamp.

"What is this figure?" Ibn Battuta asked. He was not accustomed to seeing human beings of the Muslim faith depicted in a church.

He thought the monk replied that it was the Prophet Ali, one of the companions of Muhammad. What he may have said was Elias, which in Greek sounds something like Ali.

Ibn Battuta was pleased to hear what he thought was a familiar name and concluded that the party had made a wise choice in seeking out a building protected by a companion of Muhammad. Servants went to work to cook some chickens for a meal, but the food was no good. All the provisions had been soaked in salt water.

It behooved the travelers to move at once to a place where they could obtain fresh supplies. They had landed on the southeast side of the Crimean peninsula, and the nearest city was Feodosiya. One of the merchants succeeded in hiring a horse-drawn wagon, and they all got in with him and traveled in that direction. Ibn Battuta was warned that Feodosiya was mostly a Christian city, inhabited by Genoese, so he was much relieved at the sight of a Muslim mosque. Here he arranged quarters for himself and his companions close by. They had been in the place only an hour when he heard bells ringing on every side.

Now Muslim tradition said, "The angels will not enter in any house in which bells are rung," so Ibn Battuta, never having been close to such a brazen violation of the rules of his faith, at once ordered the members of his party to ascend the minaret and chant the Koran and the call to prayer.

The words had barely blared forth from the platform around the top of the minaret when a man rushed into the mosque. He wore a breastplate and brandished a sword.

Ibn Battuta met him and demanded, "What is your business here?"

The man put away his sword. "I am the kadi of the Muslims of Feodosiya, and when I heard the call to prayer I feared for your safety and came to your aid, as you see," he explained. "This city has a large Christian population, and you might precipitate trouble unless you call your people down and stop them from chanting up there."

The Moor hastened to follow his advice, relieved that he had made contact so soon with a man who understood Arabic.

Amidst the din of the bells, no one else seemed to have noticed the cries from the minaret, and no harm resulted. The travelers saw that they must modify their customs and conform with those of the surrounding population, then they would be left in peace. They were assured that in most of the country they would find Tatars who were a Turkish people, Muslims, of course, but here in Feodosiya the Genoese were dominant. The two groups got along well with each other, and Ibn Battuta was told he was free to wander in the bazaars and visit the port where two hundred vessels, large and small, were anchored.

He and his companions made arrangements for another wagon to carry them to Kiram, about twenty-six miles to the west, where a Tatar emir governed the district for the powerful Sultan Muhammad Uzbeg Khan.

Not quite a hundred years earlier the Golden Horde, led by a grandson of Genghiz Khan, had raided eastern Europe, and when the Mongols were defeated in battle a few years later, they retreated to the Volga River, built their "Golden Camp" at its mouth and established the realm which Ibn Battuta was about to visit. Sultan Uzbeg's people had succeeded the Golden Horde and were known as the Blue Horde. They were an outgrowth of the great invasion, although there were few Mongols among them, mostly Tatars.

Word of the arrival of the pilgrim traveler already had reached the emir at Kiram, and he sent Ibn Battuta a horse, a gift which reassured the Moor of his welcome. He felt at ease, for he was able to communicate with these people, having acquired enough knowledge of Turkish words during his year in Asia Minor. When he arrived at the Tatar city, he was given lodging at the hospice of a prominent sheikh. All boded well for the continuation of the journey, as the emir was about to set out for the sultan's capital, and he invited Ibn Battuta to travel in his company.

This was to be a journey of considerable length across the southern Ukraine and the land that separated the Sea of Azov and the Caspian Sea. There were no means of travel except by clumsy wagons called arabas. They had four large wheels, and on the wagon bed was a structure called a yurt, similar to the tent Ibn Battuta had stayed in on the mountain at Birgi. It consisted of a lath cupola tied together with thin strips of hide and covered with felt in which were grilled windows, so that the person inside could look out without being seen. He would thus have the privacy of a room on wheels in which to employ himself as he pleased, sleeping, eating, reading, or writing. The driver rode outside on one of the horses. Wagons were pulled by oxen, camels, or horses. There were extra tent wagons to carry the baggage, and these could be locked.

Ibn Battuta, who had come out of Turkey well provided with funds from the many gifts of the sultans he had visited, hired several vehicles: a wagon for himself and a slave girl, another small wagon for the friend who had come with him all the way from Jidda, and a large wagon drawn by three camels for the rest of his party. His entourage was that of a man of consequence.

The caravan program was organized much like the camel trains of pilgrims bound for Mecca. The leader set out after dawn prayer and halted in the midforenoon, starting again after noon and halting in the evening. At each stop attendants drove the animals out to pasture. No one had to feed the beasts, for there was plenty of grazing on the desert herbage. No guards were needed for the animals because the laws against theft were severe. If a person were found with a stolen horse, he had to restore it with nine others like it; if not, his sons were taken as slaves. If he had no sons and was unable to pay, he was killed.

At mealtime Ibn Battuta had to accustom himself to new foods. Cooking was done over fires fed with animal dung. There was no other fuel on the steppes, and servants picked up the dung as they traveled along.

The Tatars prepared a dish from pounded millet, and cut small pieces of meat into the porridge when they cooked it. They poured curdled milk or mare's milk over the mixture. Another dish was a paste of eggplant or spinach and yogurt in which small pieces of meat were cut and cooked in a pot, again with curdled milk poured over the entire concoction. They had a drink made of fermented millet. They disliked sweetmeats, as the Moor later discovered. On the other hand they were permitted by their doctrine to drink millet beer. Here the Moor drew the line, for all alcoholic drinks were forbidden by his religion.

The caravan traveled eighteen days across the steppes and reached an expanse of water which the wagons were an entire day fording. This was the Miuss River west of Taganrog, near the northeastern tip of the Sea of Azov.

The emir summoned Ibn Battuta and gave him a letter to the governor of Azov, then sent him ahead of the caravan, promising that he would be treated honorably on arrival.

Azov, at the mouth of the Don River, was a starting place for caravans departing on long journeys to the interior. It was much visited by Genoese merchants, being the farthest place in Russia their vessels could reach.

Arriving two days ahead of the emir's escort, the Moor was able to observe the details of setting up camp for the deputy ruler. Three pavilions were erected, one of silk of several colors and the others of linen. They were surrounded with a cloth enclosure, and silk strips were spread on the ground for the emir to walk on when he dismounted.

The emir received the message and treated the Moor as an honored guest and asked Ibn Battuta to go ahead of him to where a settee inlaid with colored wood and topped with a magnificent cushion had been placed in the audience tent. The emir sat down on it with Ibn Battuta on one side and a sheikh on the other side. Officials came in and seated themselves on rugs close by, and the emir's sons took places standing quite near.

Servants then brought in platters of food and skins of mare's milk and beer. As soon as the feast was over, Koran readers entered the pavilion and recited. A pulpit was set up and a khoja (a Muhammadan teacher) addressed the assemblage, after which the Koran readers chanted. Hours passed, and the ceremony went on into the evening. More food was brought, after which beautiful horses were led into the tent, and the emir presented them to the notables present.

"This one is for our worthy pilgrim," he announced, and the reins were handed to Ibn Battuta.

He thanked his host, and a servant led the beautiful

animal away to the Moor's camp. So ended the emir's audience in Azov.

Horses were raised in this region in as great numbers as sheep in other lands. One Tatar might possess thousands of the animals. For every thousand he placed a small felt pennant on his wagon, and the Moor saw as many as ten of these flags on a single cart. He learned that the horses were exported in great bands to India.

The caravan proceeded on its way east and south, the Moor enjoying the long leisurely days as the yurt rolled on toward the Caucasus. He was impressed by the remarkable respect in which women were held in this country. The wife of the emir traveled in a wagon covered with rich blue woolen cloth and was attended by four beautiful, richly dressed girls. When she approached her husband's camp, she descended, and about thirty girls carried her train, holding it up by loops so that their mistress' skirts cleared the ground on every side. The wife sat down by the emir with her maidens around her. Skins of fermented mare's milk were brought in, and she knelt down and offered a bowl of the drink to her husband. Then the emir poured some for his wife. They ate food together when it was brought, and afterward he gave her an elegant robe, and she withdrew.

Ibn Battuta reflected that it would be difficult to convince his Arab friends at home that Muslim women should participate in such public gatherings and be treated with so much honor. He had observed that the Turkoman traders often traveled with a wife sitting in a wagon, with three or four girls attending her. She might wear a conical headdress adorned with precious stones and topped with waving peacock feathers. The windows of her tent were open, and her face was visible to passersby. Women went to the bazaar unveiled and accompanied by male slaves, bringing sheep and milk to exchange for spices. Sometimes a husband accompanied his wife, appearing to the Moor more like her servant than her master.

It was now toward the end of May, 1332, and the emir was

bound for a place in the foothills of the Caucasus near Pyati-
gorsk, where there were hot mineral springs. Here Sultan Muhammad Uzbeg Khan was intending to set up camp. Ibn
Battuta erected his own tent on a low hill, fixed his flag in
front of it, as was the custom of the Turks, and drew up his
horses and wagons behind. From this vantage point he
watched the ruler's camp approach, a vast city in motion, with
mosques, bazaars, and kitchens on wheels. On reaching the
designated camping place the Turks removed the tents from
the wagons and set them on the ground, doing likewise with
the mosques and the shops.

The Moor saw the sultan's wives pass by, each with her
separate retinue. The fourth wife noticed the tent on the hill
with the standard of a new arrival flying over it, and she dispatched pages and girls to salute Ibn Battuta. She halted to
await their return, and the Moor sent one of his companions
with them, bearing a gift. The sultana responded by giving
orders that the visitor was to be under her protection.

Last of all the sultan moved up and encamped. He received Ibn Battuta next day at a ceremonial audience to cele-
brate the breaking of the fast of Ramadan. It was the ruler's
custom to sit every Friday after prayers in his Gold Pavilion, its rich fabric supported by wooden rods covered with
gold plaques. In the center of this great tent was a wooden
couch adorned with silver gilt. Its legs were of pure silver,
their bases encrusted with precious stones.

The sultanas stationed themselves on either side of the
throne, and below were Uzbeg Khan's first and second sons
and a daughter. He received each of his wives formally, then
the emirs entered, a page carrying a chair for each of them.
Royal relatives were seated up front. Other persons were admitted three at a time. They saluted the ruler and retired
to sit at a distance.

When afternoon prayer ended, the sultanas and their reti-
nues retired to their wagons, each accompanied by about fifty
girls riding on horses. In front of each wagon were twenty

elderly women also riding horses, and behind the whole cortege were a hundred warriors, some on horseback and others on foot. Ibn Battuta had never witnessed such ceremonial arrays of retainers accompanying royal women. In the lands he had visited wives were never on display. Yet here was one of the seven great monarchs of the world (so Ibn Battuta rated the sultan) publicly honoring his wives.

When the Moor presented himself at the royal tent, he was invited to share a feast consisting of horseflesh, mutton, and a kind of macaroni. Ibn Battuta had in his party a man who excelled in the making of sweetmeats, so he brought along a plate of them to offer as a special treat for the sultan. This turned out to be a mistake, for instead of enjoying the candies, the ruler touched one with his finger, politely put the finger to his mouth, and signaled his servants to remove the gift. In this fashion the Moor learned that Uzbeg Khan had no taste for sweets.

Before the gathering broke up, two prominent men rose and recommended that the traveler be honored. Ibn Battuta already had learned that in this realm the Turks and Tatars did not practice the custom of giving hospitable lodging to a visitor or supplying money for his needs. Instead they made presents of sheep and horses for slaughtering as food and skins of koumiss, fermented mare's milk. Ibn Battuta was going to have to keep his wits about him to find ways to stretch his funds, but he was supremely confident that a method would show itself.

He was advised that he must pay a visit to each of the sultan's wives at her ornate tent, distinguished with a silver cupola encrusted with gold or precious stones. Everything surrounding these royal ladies was magnificent, even their horses were decked in gilt and silken cloths.

Feeling a little embarrassed that he was about to be received in a sultan's harem, Ibn Buttuta made his initial call on the principal wife, mother of the ruler's two sons. He found her seated among her ladies and wearing a small crown of jewels and peacock feathers. Her silk robe was encrusted with gems. Around her were about sixty servants and court ladies, all cleaning cherries. Those of the sultana were on a golden tray while the maidens had gold and silver salvers for their fruit.

The sultana apparently did not plan to interrupt her domestic task except to provide refreshment for the visitor. She ordered fermented mare's milk brought in, poured some into an elegant wooden bowl, and handed it herself to Ibn Battuta. He had no choice but to taste it. He found the drink bitter and disagreeable, so mindful of the sultan's own rejection of the candy, the Moor passed his drink to one of his companions.

Next day he visited the second sultana and found her reading the Koran while her ladies embroidered. She also served him koumiss, and again he pretended to sip and passed it on.

The third sultana, Bayalun, was the daughter of the emperor of Constantinople, and she was eager to hear about Ibn Battuta's journey. She served him some food, wept a little as she recalled her own homeland, and said before he left, "Do not stay away from us, but come and inform us of your needs." When Ibn Battuta returned to his tent, she sent him several kinds of foods, a quantity of bread (which was rare here), butter, sheep, money, a fine robe, three excellent horses, and ten ordinary ones.

He realized she was homesick for the West and that he had made a good impression. He knew he would also be welcome at the tent of the fourth sultana, the one who had previously taken him under her protection. He found her kind and generous and most interested in his plans to continue his journey. She served him food, meanwhile asking many questions.

While at the sultan's camp in the foothills, Ibn Battuta heard stories of the Land of Darkness far to the north, where the cold was intense and the winter days extremely short. Later when he narrated his adventures, he claimed that he had made a journey to a city midway up the Volga River, where men traded for furs—a journey that had to be taken by dog team. He could not have done so in the limited time available, and he said too little about the country to have actually seen it, but he must have listened to some true tales of northern travel while he sat through long nights in the royal camp.

He was there during Ramadan, and when the month of fasting ended, a grand festival was held, marked with feasting, singing, and drinking fermented liquors. An entire wagonload of skins containing koumiss was delivered to Ibn Battuta, and he gave it away to his Turkish neighbors. The sultan was late at Friday prayers, and some courtiers said drunkenness had got the best of him. He appeared in due time, swaying on his feet and smiling broadly.

The royal caravan moved on to the city of Astrakhan on the Volga River, where the sultan always resided until it was cold enough for the stream to freeze over. On arrival at this metropolis north of the Caspian Sea, the Sultana Bayalun pleaded with Uzbeg Khan to permit her to return to Constantinople for the coming birth of her child. She wanted to be in her father's palace for this event.

When the sultan gave his consent, Ibn Battuta was inspired to ask permission to accompany the sultana's expedition. He had always wished to see the great Greek city, and this seemed like a wonderful opportunity, although it would mean retracing a long distance across the steppes.

"No," the sultan told him. "I will not consent. It will be too dangerous for you, a Muslim."

Ibn Battuta replied, "O sultan, if I visit Constantinople under your protection and patronage I shall have nothing to fear from anyone."

Sultan Uzbeg Khan reconsidered. He did not keep Ibn Battuta long in suspense.

"Very well," he said, "you shall go in the royal caravan."

With that decision he sent the Moor a handsome gift consisting of a robe, a large number of horses, and 1,500 dinars in gold coins. Each of the sultanas also sent presents of silver ingots, and the sultan's daughter gave him money, a robe, and another horse. Altogether he was very presentably supplied for the journey. He took along some sable and miniver (vair, or Siberian squirrel) furs to trade.

The calvalcade set out on July 5, 1332, the sultan escorting Bayalun the first day and the other wives remaining through the second day. An emir with five thousand troops went along, as well as the sultana's troops numbering about five hundred, of whom two hundred were Greeks and slaves. She was accompanied by about two hundred slave girls, mostly Greeks, ten Greek pages, ten Indian pages, four hundred wagons, two thousand horses, three hundred oxen, and two hundred camels, so there was a large company on this journey across the vast plains.

It is difficult to follow the route of the cavalcade, as Ibn Battuta in telling of it later did not mention many place names. After passing near the Sea of Azov and the silver mines of the Miuss River, it crossed the Lower Dneiper River in the Ukraine, arriving at the last of the Turkish towns. From here on the travelers were in Greek territory, the first eighteen days through an uninhabited wasteland. For eight days water had to be carried in skins on the wagons. The weather was cool, and the travelers experienced no thirst. The Turks in any case carried milk in large skins, mixing it with their millet porridge and drinking it.

Ibn Battuta never told how he crossed such great rivers as the Dneiper and the mouth of the Danube. He spoke of waiting for the ebb at a tidal river and fording it where it was two miles in width, then traveling through sands four miles and fording again for three miles, then two miles among rocks and finally reaching a third channel a mile wide. The entire breadth of this delta was twelve miles, and some boats must have been used to cross the open water.

Word of Bayalun's approach had reached the Greeks, and a body of troops joined her at a castle in Bulgaria, also ladies of the court and nurses. From there it was twenty-two days' travel to Constantinople. The wagons were left behind, and all took to riding horses and mules through mountainous country. Sultana Bayalun sent Ibn Battuta six mules for this purpose. He left his slaves and companions behind to care for the baggage which was put in a house assigned to them.

Only the sultana's own people traveled with her from this point, the emir turning back with his troops. The portable mosque was also left behind at the castle, and the call to prayer was discontinued. The Moor was keenly aware that he was entering a completely alien land from which had once come Crusaders whose aim was to wrest the Near East from the followers of Muhammad. By any interpretation an Arab visitor stood for "enemy" in Christian eyes.

Ibn Battuta had to become accustomed to sights that shocked him. Wines were brought, and the sultana drank them. Not only that, he was told, she ate pork. No one remained with her to observe the Muslim prayers except one Turk, who prayed daily with the Moor.

In spite of the changed surroundings, the sultana, true to her promises, ordered that Ibn Battuta must be treated honorably. On one occasion a soldier was ordered beaten after he laughed at seeing the Moor bowing toward Mecca to pray.

After the cavalcade had traveled some distance, the sultana's brother and five thousand horsemen, bristling with arms, arrived on the scene. He rode beneath a jeweled parasol and was accompanied by standards, horses laden with armament, kettledrums, other parasols, trumpets, bugles, and flutes. Bayalun, clad in a jeweled mantle, rode out to greet him. She was on a horse with a silk saddlecloth embroidered in gold, gold anklets on its feet, necklaces of precious stones, and a jewel-encrusted saddle.

Next day the procession encamped on the outskirts of a large coastal city, and another brother, who was heir to the throne, came out with ten thousand mailed men.

The sultana's escort made a final camp ten miles outside

Constantinople, where thousands of persons on foot greeted her. Next to arrive were the emperor and empress and imperial musicians. Horsemen carried a canopy over the emperor's head, and men on foot marched before him, carrying long staves.

Ibn Battuta, fearing for his life among the mob of unbelievers gathered to greet the sultana, remained with the party guarding her baggage. Amid a cloud of dust and the ringing of church bells, the cortege entered the city. At length the group the Moor was with reached the first gates of the palace, where a hundred men stood guard. Some called out, "Saracens, Saracens!" and Ibn Battuta was barred from entry.

One of the escort said, "They came with the sultana."

The reply was "They cannot enter except by permission."

So the whole party remained at the gate while a messenger was sent to inform Sultana Bayalun, who was still with her father.

Soon the messenger was back with an order to admit the Muslims and assign them a house near Bayalun's residence. In addition, the emperor had written that they were not to be molested wherever they went, and this was proclaimed in the streets and in the bazaars.

Nevertheless, Ibn Battuta hesitated to go out and remained in the house three nights. There he received hospitality gifts of flour, bread, sheep, fowls, butter, fruit, fish, money, and rugs. On the fourth day Emperor Andronicus III summoned the Moor to an audience, and Sumbul, the sultana's Indian page, escorted the Muslim visitor to Blachernae Palace in the northwestern part of the capital. They passed through four gates, each with porticoes at which stood armed foot soldiers. At a fifth gate Sumbul left the guest and returned with four pages who searched Ibn Battuta to make certain he carried no knife.

The officer apologized, explaining, "This is the custom. Every person who enters the emperor's presence, be he noble or commoner, foreign or native, must be searched."

Then the officer took Ibn Battuta by the hand and opened the door. Two men caught his sleeves, and two more walked behind him while they entered a large hall adorned with pictures of people and animals. In the center was a water channel with trees on either side and men standing around, no one speaking.

In so solemn a setting and so completely guarded, Ibn Battuta felt like a prisoner taken in an unfought battle. He was delivered to three other men, who seized hold of his garments and on a signal led him forward, as though to his execution.

A voice beside him said in Arabic, "Do not be afraid, for this is their custom, and they use it with every visitor."

Ibn Battuta was comforted by hearing a familiar tongue. "I am a Jew," the man explained, "and I will be your interpreter. I am originally from Syria."

"How shall I salute the emperor?" Ibn Battuta asked.

"Say *al-salamu alaikum*, as is your custom," the man counseled.

They entered a great pavilion where the emperor sat on his throne with the empress close by and the sultana and her brothers in front. Several armed men stood on either side.

The emperor seemed aware that the Moor had not recovered from his alarm at being so closely guarded. He signaled his guest to sit down until his apprehension was calmed. In a few moments Ibn Battuta recovered his composure. He rose, approached, and saluted the emperor. With the Jew acting as interpreter, the ruler asked questions about affairs in Jerusalem, the appearance of the Sacred Rock, the Church of the Holy Sepulchre, the cradle of Jesus, and Bethlehem. He also wanted to know what Ibn Battuta had observed in Hebron, Damascus, Cairo, Iraq, and the land of Rum.

It was a lengthy conversation, and the emperor appeared pleased with his guest's knowledgeable replies. Turning to his sons, he said, "Honor this man and ensure his safety while he is here."

Then he had a robe of honor brought for Ibn Battuta and ordered for him a saddled and bridled horse and a royal parasol, to indicate that he was under the emperor's protection.

"I have a request," said Ibn Battuta in thanking him. "Would you kindly designate someone to ride about the city with me every day, that I may see its wonders and curious sights in order to be able to tell about them in my own country."

The emperor granted his wish, and Ibn Battuta had the unique experience of being paraded under the parasol through the bazaars to the accompaniment of trumpets, fifes, and drums, so that all might see the visitor. He was escorted to the Golden Horn to view its boats and to Galata, where a hundred merchant ships were anchored. His guides took him to the great church of Aya Sofia, but he was not allowed beyond the courtyard, which he entered with the emperor's father, who had abdicated the throne and become a monk. Ibn Battuta met him while riding on the bank of a river where the former emperor was walking on foot, wearing haircloth garments and a felt bonnet. The Greek guide, who knew Arabic, ordered the Moor to dismount and salute the emperor's father, who was accompanied by other monks.

The ex-emperor told the guide, "Say to this Saracen I clasp the hand that has entered Jerusalem and the foot that has walked within the Dome of the Rock and the great Church of the Holy Sepulchre and Bethlehem."

As he spoke these words he placed a hand on Ibn Battuta's feet. The Muslim traveler was amazed at this holy man's belief in the merits of one who, though not of his religion, had entered hallowed places.

The former emperor then took the visitor's hand, and as the pair walked along Ibn Battuta answered questions about Jerusalem and what he had seen of the Christians living there. When they reached the courtyard of Aya Sofia, the old man let go of the traveler's hand, saying to the guide, "Tell him that everyone who enters this door must need prostrate himself before the great cross. It is a rule laid down by the ancients and cannot be contravened."

Thus they parted, and Ibn Battuta did not see the old man again.

After a month had passed, it became clear to the Turks in Sultana Bayalun's company that she professed her father's religion and wished to remain with him, so they asked permission to return to their country. The Moor had fulfilled his dream of seeing Constantinople and was ready to go. They were another week preparing for the trip, as they were to have an escort of five hundred horsemen. The sultana sent for Ibn Battuta and gave him three hundred dinars in Greek gold coins, two thousand Venetian dirhems, a length of hand-worked woolen cloth, ten robes of silk, linen, and wool, and two horses. She said some of these things were gifts from her father.

On October 24, 1332, the party set out for the frontier, where they had left their associates and wagons. They were escorted to a border city, then the Greek troops departed. Winter weather had set in on the steppes, and Ibn Battuta sometimes dressed in three fur coats, two pairs of trousers, one of them quilted, woolen boots with quilted boots on top of them and leather ones on the outside. He performed his ablutions close to the fire, using heated water. If he dowsed his face in cold water, his beard would freeze. If his nose ran, the drops froze on his moustache. He was not used to being so cold and so bundled up. He wore so much clothing, he had to be helped to mount his horse.

The caravan retraced its course, going 225 miles north of Astrakhan to where the sultan was now in his capital. It was necessary to travel three nights on the frozen surface of the Volga River. Whenever water was needed, servants cut pieces of ice and melted them in a caldron for drinking and cooking purposes.

On the fourth day of traveling up the river, they reached the capital, called al-Sara (or Sarai, near present Volgograd, ex-Stalingrad). The sultan sent for Ibn Battuta, asking him how the journey had gone and what were his impressions of the Greeks and Constantinople. The ruler then ordered all supplies Ibn Battuta needed for his party's maintenance.

Al-Sara was a huge city spread over twenty square miles of the plain, and it took Ibn Battuta an entire day to ride a circuit around it, stopping for noon prayer and to eat. It took half a day to walk across the metropolis and back, always through a continuous line of houses. The population was made up of various groups of people, including some Christians, each group having a separate quarter and its own shops. Ibn Battuta, always checking on matters of religion, counted thirteen mosques in al-Sara.

Having made his hoped-for side trip to Constantinople, Ibn Battuta was anxious to be on his way toward India. A large caravan was preparing to depart for Khwarizm (now Kunya Urgench, a town in Turkmen, U.S.S.R., just south of the Aral Sea on the river Amu Darya), among which were some merchants of his acquaintance. He made an agreement to travel with them, for this was no country to attempt to penetrate with a small party. Ahead of the travelers, between al-Sara and Khwarizm, lay a desert of forty days' march, which only camels could travel, and these were the animals that henceforth would draw the wagons.

VII
The Road to Samarkand and India

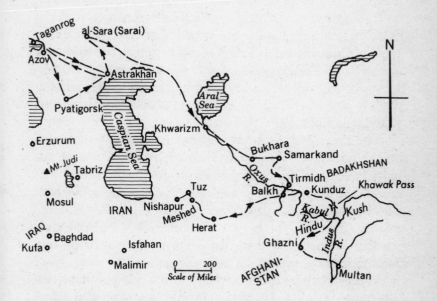

The lands which lay ahead of Ibn Battuta on the next lap of
his journey to India had been inhabited in extremely ancient
days and had once been considered the garden spot of the
world. However, the Mongols had swept over them in the
previous century and left desolation behind. Most of the country had never recovered from the scourge of the invading
hordes.

Ibn Battuta, led by his insatiable curiosity, again had to
adapt to new conditions. His finances were in a comfortable
state, and he had a household consisting of three slave girls
to care for his personal wants and keep him company.

He sold his horses near the mouth of the Ural River at the
head of the Caspian Sea, where there was a bridge of boats

somewhat like the one he had seen in Baghdad. Here he hired camels, and the expedition continued by forced marches toward the southern end of the Aral Sea. The travelers halted an hour in the forenoon, and another hour at sunset, only long enough to cook millet porridge and mutton and eat it. The mixture was brought to a boil just once, then pieces of dried meat were dropped into it and sour milk poured over the top. Everyone ate and slept in the wagons while they were on the move. Watering places were two or three days' journey apart, the precious liquid being taken from rainwater pools or shallow wells in the sand. There was almost no herbage on which the camels could graze.

With the end of the desert the caravan arrived at Khwarizm on the river Amu Darya, the Oxus of antiquity, one of the most fabled streams of the universe (to Ibn Battuta it was one of the four rivers of Paradise). The city lay in an oasis dependent upon the stream for irrigation. Ibn Battuta considered Khwarizm the largest, most beautiful, and most important metropolis of the Asiatic Turks, for it had splendid bazaars, broad streets, and a huge population.

He separated from the caravan at this place and at first camped on the outskirts of the city and sent word to the kadi of his arrival. Since he was still in Sultan Uzbeg's territory, he knew he could expect to be well received.

A man came to guide his party next day to a newly built college. As the building was not yet occupied, the kadi suggested that they make use of it.

When the Moor went out to look at Khwarizm, he found crowds so dense in the shopping streets he gave up trying to ride among them. The people were extremely friendly to strangers and very pious. If they did not appear at prayer, the muezzins (men whose duty it was to call the faithful to prayer from the minaret of a mosque) went to the houses and routed them out. When a man failed to attend the mosque service, he was fined and sometimes punished with a beating.

The kadi received the traveler at his house, furnished richly with carpets, the walls hung with brocades and embroideries. There were many niches to display silver-gilt vessels and Iraqi glass. After enduring desert fare, Ibn Battuta enjoyed the bountiful meals served by the Muslim judge. They went together to visit the ruling emir, who was ill with gout. He sat on a silk rug with a cover over his legs while he questioned Ibn Battuta about Sultan Uzbeg, the Sultana Bayalun, and her father in Constantinople. The men had much to talk about while a feast was brought in by the emir's servants.

The provincial ruler expressed his pleasure in the Moor's visit by sending him at the college gifts of rice, flour, sheep, butter, spices, and firewood. Some days later he sent five hundred dirhems and commanded that a banquet costing another five hundred dirhems be prepared in the traveler's honor, to which would be invited sheikhs, doctors of law, and principal citizens.

The Moor, having learned that it did not profit him to remain silent about his circumstances, went boldly to the governor and protested, "O emir, you are preparing a banquet at which those present will eat only a mouthful or two. If you were to give me the amount of money you spend for the feast, it would be far more useful to me."

"I shall do so," the emir told him and shortly afterward dispatched a page with a purse containing the remainder of the sum. That very day Ibn Battuta purchased a black horse and paid for it out of the money. Although he acquired many horses in the course of his travels, this was his favorite, and he kept it three years. He said of the animal, "When it died, my affairs took a turn for the worse."

After all there was a banquet for the traveler, given by the sister of the emir's wife in a hospice she had built, where food was supplied to wayfarers. At this feast Ibn Battuta was presented with a sable cloak and another excellent horse.

He did not see the donor, but as he departed from the

hospice, he came face to face with a woman at the gate who was wearing soiled garments and a veil over her head. She greeted him, he replied politely but did not pay any more attention to her. Then after he had gone a little distance, someone overtook him and said the woman was his hostess. Covered with confusion, Ibn Battuta went back to speak with her, but she had already gone, so he sent his apologies through one of his attendants. He always was exceptionally careful about the social amenities.

On leaving Khwarizm there was no more traveling in the houses on wheels. He purchased a double litter, one side to be occupied by a companion. He hired additional camels and his servants rode some of the horses. Another sandy desert had to be crossed, eighteen days march to Bukhara (in present Usbek, U.S.S.R.). Six of those days there were no watering places.

Formerly Bukhara had been the capital of the lands beyond the Oxus River, but it had been laid in ruins by Genghiz Khan in 1220 and sacked twice again by the Mongol khans from Persia, the last time in 1316. Little was left of the great city, and Ibn Battuta regretted that of the remaining population no one seemed interested in religious learning. He took the trouble at this place to visit a cemetery and copy a number of noteworthy inscriptions on the old Muslim tombs.

As the party moved on up the river valley toward Samarkand, Ibn Battuta was due for a fresh experience. He was about to become a father by one of his slave girls. At Nasaf, where the sultan of Turkestan was encamped, he sent her ahead toward the town by camel litter, and when he got in, he had to dispatch servants to search for her party. He had permission to camp close to a mosque, and the sultan's deputy (the ruler was away on a hunting expedition) sent him a felt tent where the blessed event took place that night. The baby was a daughter. Ibn Battuta never said much about her except that she died two months after his arrival in India.

The sultan returned to his camp after some days, and Ibn Battuta was presented to him at the mosque. The ruler invited the Moor to his audience hall in a great tent lined with silken cloth of gold, where he sat in a chair resembling a pulpit. It was covered with gold-embroidered silk, and overhead hung a jeweled crown. Seated around the sultan were courtiers, behind them were soldiers with weapons, and nearby were the ruler's sons waving fly whisks. When Ibn Battuta entered, four courtiers rose to greet him, and another came forward to act as interpreter.

The sultan asked many questions about Mecca, Medina, Jerusalem, Damascus, Cairo, Iraq, and other places. After that the Moor frequently attended prayer services in the ruler's company. Although it was a season of intense cold, he never failed to appear, the sultan joking when he was late at the mosque.

Sultan Tarmashirin was a good-natured man, and Ibn Battuta was loath to leave the vicinity of his camp. He remained nearly two months, enjoying his role as a new father, for he remarked that his little girl was born under a lucky star. "From that time on," he said, "I experienced everything to give me joy and satisfaction."

Early in May, 1333, he decided to resume his travels, and, hearing this, the sultan gave him seven hundred silver dinars and a valuable sable coat, two horses, and two camels. It was a bitterly cold day when the Moor said good-bye to the sultan at his hunting ground. "I was so chilled I could say nothing," he recalled, "but Sultan Tarmashirin understood. He laughed, gave me his hand and said farewell."

Ibn Battuta's party continued on the way to Samarkand, still a beautiful place, though most of the city was in ruins. Waterwheels along the river irrigated the orchards, and there was a promenade with benches beside the stream and booths, where fruits and other edibles were sold. The travelers lodged at a hospice adjoining a famous jeweled tomb, then they went on to Tirmidh on the Amu Darya, where Ibn Battuta was astonished to see the bathhouses supplied with jars of milk. Each man entering was supposed to take a small jug of it and wash his head.

Next stop on the way was after crossing another desert to reach ancient Balkh, in northern Afghanistan. In the distance it had the appearance of an occupied city, but Ibn Battuta found it completely ruined and uninhabited. He went around looking at the inscriptions in blue paint the color of lapis lazuli that still survived on mosques and colleges. (Balkh was so old its people called it the Mother of Cities. It was sacked by Genghiz Khan in 1220.)

Desiring not to miss any famous places in the region, Ibn Battuta turned west again to Herat (in present Afhganistan) and Meshed (in present Iran). From the latter city he went to a shrine at nearby Tuz, which held the tomb of Harun al-Rashid, the caliph of the Arabian Nights stories, who died there in 809 while on the expedition.

Ibn Battuta had crossed into Iran, and while at Nishapur he purchased a Turkish slave boy. The sheikh who was his host at a hospice declared, "This boy is no good to you. Sell him."

The Moor followed this advice and rejoiced that he did so, for afterward he learned that the slave killed another person, and for this crime he was put to death.

Back in the upper Oxus River valley and inside the country of Badakhshan, Ibn Battuta stopped for forty days to rest his camels and horses near Kunduz (in present Afghanistan) and wait for the best time to cross through the snow of the Hindu Kush mountains into India. This range, which separates the Oxus and the Indus River valleys, is so high and dangerous that its name meant "Slayer of Indians," the Moor was told. Once more he was launched on a terrific adventure, the like of which he had never previously experienced.

There was no other way to cross the mountain barrier except

through one of the high passes, which were not far below the line of perpetual snow. At length the travelers were ready to take their chances on surmounting the summit. They entered the valley leading upward to Khawak Pass, which lay at 11,640-feet elevation. For an entire day men went ahead of the camels, spreading cloths for them to walk on so that they should not sink into the deep snow. Although the travelers had waited for warm weather and set out at dawn, they were still struggling along in the late afternoon, and they were not over the pass until after sunset. The combination of exposure to ice and sun had given Ibn Battuta a bad sunburn, a condition he had not thought possible for a man from a desert land.

The party came out of the high mountains by a silver-mine town on a tributary of the Kabul River. (They had taken a roundabout route. Most crossings of the mountain range in modern times are by the Khyber Pass and into the Indus Valley.) They were in country where rubies were found, but the Moor was less interested in gems than in a saintly man they met while encamped near a hospice. Although he looked only fifty years of age, he claimed to be 350 years old. He insisted that with the passing of every century he grew new hair and teeth. Ibn Battuta doubted how much truth there was in his claims.

Beyond Ghazni (in present Afghanistan) the travelers had to pass a fortress between two mountains, where Afghans were in the habit of intercepting travelers in the narrow defile. This was still in high country and uneasiness prevailed. The party might yet not make it through to safer realms. Most Afghans, Ibn Battuta was informed, were brigands eager to waylay caravans. He did not dare make this passage without reinforcement, so he joined a group of men driving four thousand horses toward India.

As the travelers approached the defile, they spied Afghans posted on the lower slopes, waiting to attack. Members of the caravan took the initiative and shot arrows at the robbers. In the scrimmage Ibn Battuta and several others became separated from the main caravan. There was nothing they could do but make a run for it. The Moor kicked his horse, bent low over the animal, and made a dash straight through his assailants and down the road. It was no time to think of baggage and the tired camels they had been herding along. The men had dumped everything and made a run for it.

With relief they left the Afghan attackers behind. Next morning an armed party of horsemen returned and picked up the lost loads.

Many days later Ibn Battuta was finally out of the last of the Turkish and Tatar lands and prepared to try his fortunes in the realm of the powerful Sultan Muhammad Shah of India. There was an element of danger in entering his country, for the sultan had a reputation for doing away with anyone who caused his displeasure. Life was cheap in Sind and Hind, as that part of the world was then known, also admittance to enter was not easily granted. On the other hand, rewards were rich for learned men who could be of service to the country, and this was what had attracted the Moor. He had heard about the wealth of India ever since his first pilgrimage to Mecca, and he had an overwhelming desire to find out if all the reports about it were true.

Since the sultan was a Muslim, although his country was populated mostly by infidels, Ibn Battuta foresaw that a scholarly pilgrim might be welcome. He had taken risks before, and now he was amply advised how to meet the entrance requirements. He couldn't know that these would prove his undoing.

VIII
In Debt in Delhi

When Ibn Battuta reached a frontier town on the Indus River in September, 1333, he encountered intelligence officers stationed there for the purpose of writing down the circumstances of all new arrivals and reporting them to the sultan. The information they collected was sent first to the governor in the city of Multan (in present Punjab, Pakistan) and then would be forwarded to Delhi by a remarkable horse postal service. Normally the journey between the two places required fifty days, but the post was carried by couriers running short relays day and night, which made it possible for a letter to travel the distance in five days.

The intelligence officers wrote down a full description of the appearance and dress of each traveler, the number in his party, how many slaves, servants, and beasts accompanied him, how he behaved on the road and while at rest in the town, and how he passed his time. The man's background did not matter. Only the actions and conduct of a foreigner were noted.

Every arrival had to have a gift ready to present to the ruler in person. The sultan, it was understood, would eventually return many times the present's value. Merchants of the border country did an unusual type of business, supplying new arrivals with generous loans and whatever the newcomer desired to offer as a gift. The idea was that when the traveler received his benefaction from the sultan, the obligations would be paid off, and the merchant would reap a large profit from his investment.

This arrangement suited the Moor well enough. He was inexperienced in business matters and accustomed to having his finances adjust themselves through some bounty received along the way. He borrowed heavily from the merchants and, having been informed what types of gift were suitable to offer the sultan, he bought lavishly: camels, horses, white slaves, and especially a camel load of arrows, which had some extraordinary significance.

The sultan's officers permitted him to proceed as far as Multan, where he was to await Muhammad Shah's order as to what degree of hospitality would be extended to him. On the way the route led through a forest of reeds near the Indus River, and here the Moor saw his first rhinoceros when the bulky animal came out of a thicket, struck a horse, piercing the mount's thigh with its horn, and then retired again to the jungle.

On the way to Multan a part of the prophecy about Ibn Battuta's voyages was realized. He met a learned sheikh, the first whom the holy men he had visited at Alexandria had predicted he would encounter and to whom he was to carry greetings. The prediction seemed beyond belief back in Egypt, yet the Moor had crossed a large section of the world and now encountered one of the very persons he had considered himself most unlikely to find. If the prophecy had validity, he believed, then he really was destined to be admitted to India and go on to China.

At Multan Ibn Battuta experienced misgivings about coming to this land. The chief emir of the city had a bloodthirsty reputation and had just engaged in a fight with some rebellious troops. When they surrendered, he executed the leaders, cut off their heads and stacked them in the middle of the town, flayed their bodies, and hung the skins on a wall. The very first night the Moor was in Multan, it was extremely hot, and he slept on the roof of a college that had offered lodging. Waking during the early morning hours, he saw these skins attached to crosses, and the sight so filled him with horror he could not bear to remain any longer in the building.

While he waited for word as to whether the sultan would admit him to Delhi, Ibn Battuta found an opportunity to make a side trip. A judge from Khorasan had been appointed governor of a province that is now part of Pakistan and was about to sail down the Indus River with fifteen vessels that were carrying his baggage and retinue to the new post. One boat had a sheltered platform where the governor sat with his suite, soldiers around them and forty men rowing. To right and left were four vessels with standards, kettledrums, trumpets, bugles, and reed pipes. Two carried singers.

The jurist, having found Ibn Battuta an entertaining addition to his party, invited the Moor to accompany him to his capital at the port of Lahari, twenty-eight miles southeast of Karachi. When the traveler boarded the craft, his curiosity about so many accompanying musicians was quickly gratified, for almost at once they began to play. First there would be an interlude of instrumental numbers, then there would be singing, and after that once again the instruments. This kept up continuously from early morning until noon, so that Ibn Battuta always heard the oars dipping to the sound of oriental melodies played in the distance.

At midday the ships drew together, the musicians boarded the governor's boat and sang until after the meal was served, then they went back to their own craft, and the music continued in the same manner until nightfall. At dark camp was set up on the riverbank, another meal was spread, then after evening prayer sentries were posted, and the notables went to tents to sleep.

Ibn Battuta remained five days at Lahari, then the governor gave him traveling provisions, and he returned upriver to Multan. The day after his arrival the postmaster, who had written the report on the Moor, took him to call on the governor. Ibn Battuta was careful to carry gifts for this dignitary, as it was expected of him. He brought along a horse, a white slave, and a parcel of raisins and almonds, neither of which grew in India.

By this time the governor had received his orders about Ibn Battuta and instructed that his party was to be lodged in a certain house. There the Moor waited again to learn the sultan's wishes. After two months of anxious dallying a pair of officials called on him and asked, "Why have you come to India?"

"To enter permanently in the service of the Master of the World," Ibn Battuta answered.

He had been advised that this was what he should say. He was warned in advance that no one was allowed to enter the country who did not declare he intended to remain the rest of his life. Ibn Battuta had no plans, so he was willing to risk making this pledge. He had come so far and spent so many years trying to reach India he was not going to be turned back at its gate. If he desired to leave later on, he was confident he could find a way without breaking his word. He saw that some of his companions refused to take the pledge and were turned back. He didn't want this to happen to him.

The officials made everything final. They summoned a kadi and notaries and drew up a formal contract which each person remaining in the country was required to sign.

A large group of new arrivals had assembled at Multan, and they were to journey together to the sultan's capital. The trip would require nearly a month and a half and would be through country well populated, but almost entirely inhabited by infidels. Rebel bands were quite likely to attack travelers in the mountains.

A chamberlain went ahead of the caravan every day and set up the night's camp. With him went twenty cooks to provide the meals. Every traveler slept in his own tent.

One day Ibn Battuta lagged behind the rest in a group of Arabs, Persians, and Turks, who had made a late start and were some distance from the main party. Suddenly the laggards were surrounded by eighty natives on foot, accompanied by two horsemen. An arrow struck Ibn Battuta, and another hit his horse during the battle that followed. By good fortune in each case the blow was slight, and no injury resulted. A fellow traveler had his horse badly wounded, but the party captured one of the infidel mounts and gave it to the man. The Turks in the expedition killed the wounded animal and ate its flesh, as was their custom. It was a gory battle, and some of the party insisted on carrying the heads of a dozen slain infidels to the castle that was to be their destination for the day. On reaching it about midnight they suspended their bloody trophies from the wall. Ibn Battuta was revolted by these sanguinary customs. He lived in a rough age and had looked often on death, but here in India life seemed to have less value than elsewhere. Only the next day he witnessed the burning of a widow at her husband's funeral pyre. Whenever he saw one of these ceremonies, so common in India, he nearly fainted of revulsion.

Weeks of travel brought the party at length to within ten miles of Delhi, the largest Islamic city in the East. A sheikh, a doctor, and a chamberlain from the court served as official greeters to receive the caravan, acting in behalf of the sultan, who was absent from his capital.

Delhi had twenty-eight gates in its surrounding walls, which were so thick they contained granaries and space for horsemen and infantry to march from one end to the other. Windows were cut in the walls on the town side. Ibn Battuta promptly paid a visit to the cathedral mosque, noting its thirteen domes and four courts. In its center was an iron pillar he measured with a length of turban cloth and found to be approximately twelve feet around. It was said to have been from a temple to an infidel god, Vishnu, which had formerly occupied the ground. In the southern court was a tall red-stone minaret which he believed had no parallel in Islam. Another larger but unfinished minaret was in another part of the mosque, and the Moor climbed it for a view of the city. High up there, the people below looked to be no more than children.

Ibn Battuta had yet to meet the sultan, the most powerful and feared ruler he encountered in all his travels. Muhammad Shah was celebrated equally for the giving of lavish gifts and the frequent shedding of blood. Always, the Moor learned, the ruler was either enriching some poor man or executing someone who displeased him, a combination of generosity, cruelty, and violence. Ibn Battuta was keenly aware he must make a good impression from the start. A great deal was at stake, his future career, a living for himself and his now considerable household—and also repayment to his merchant creditors.

In the sultan's absence, his grand vizier held audience for the new arrivals in a room of the palace called the Thousand Pillars. Ibn Battuta was escorted through a series of three doors before reaching this great hall, where he was expected to make obeisance by touching the ground with the head or the fingers. The vizier then took him and the other visitors to the residence of the sultan's blind mother, each carrying a gift for her. A clerk at the gate listed the presents one by one in a businesslike manner. Eunuchs guarded the place and acted as messengers. Ibn Battuta had been standing waiting for some time when the eunuchs reentered and said the guests should seat themselves at two long tables in an arcade. Food was brought, and they were served from gold pitchers and plates. When the Moor was through eating, they were invited into another room and given silk robes embroidered in gold thread.

Next they were escorted to the palace gate and a chest containing lengths of silken, linen, and cotton fabrics was brought out. The Moor received a portion of these wares, after which more refreshments were brought on. The vizier, observing that Ibn Battuta was a little confused about court etiquette at this point, showed him how to do homage; placing a platter of sweets on his shoulder with one hand, he must touch the other hand to the ground at the same time. He said the Moor's party were to go to a mansion prepared for their occupancy and that hospitality gifts would be sent there.

The house proved to be well furnished with carpets, mats, utensils, and beds of a type that Ibn Battuta had not seen before. They had four legs and four wooden crosspieces crisscrossed with interwoven braids of strong cotton. With each bed went two mattresses, pillows, and a silk coverlet. These had linen or cotton slips that could be removed and washed.

In the evening a miller and a butcher brought supplies to the house, ordered by the sultan's mother. Next day Ibn Battuta and his companions again saluted the vizier at the sultan's palace and received two purses, each containing a thousand silver dinars, also a fine mohair robe. A clerk questioned the Moor about his servants, companions, and slave boys, a total of forty altogether in his party. The information was written down, and sums were provided for each person, making a total of another four thousand dinars. Methodically the court officers portioned out more gifts of provisions, such as flour, meat, sugar, and butter.

Six weeks after Ibn Battuta's arrival, his small daughter

died, and the burial was taken out of his hands. The vizier gave orders as to where the child should be buried and how. It was the custom after three days to place flowers and fruits on the tomb. Carpets were spread, the Koran was recited, servants brought julep to drink, rose water was sprinkled on all who came, and betel nuts were passed around to be chewed, a custom of the country. The kadi recited an elegy and then launched into a eulogy about the sultan, whereupon everybody rose and did homage. This ceremony honoring his dead infant amazed Ibn Battuta. It concluded with rose water being sprinkled on all present and cups of sherbet handed around. Finally eleven robes of honor were brought for Ibn Battuta and his companions. After it was over, all rode to the sultan's palace with the chamberlain, and they did homage to the throne once more. The final gesture was the arrival of more food sent to the house by the sultan's mother. A few days later her eunuchs brought a litter with silk curtains for the slave girl whose child had died. She was to go to the sultana's palace for a visit.

The young bereaved mother remained there all night and was given a thousand silver dinars, gold and jeweled bracelets, a gold crescent, and a chest of gold-embroidered silk clothing. She was not destined to keep these gifts. Ibn Battuta sent most of them to his merchant creditors, who were by then insistently reminding him that he was in their debt. He knew the royal intelligence service was reporting to the sultan concerning every move he made.

He was still feeling his way through the intricacies of court procedure when he received an indication that all was going well—an order assigning him the income from a group of villages sixteen miles out of Delhi. He rode out to view them and learned they would produce five thousand dinars annually. However, his creditors were not going to wait for this money, and it was a small amount by comparison with what he owed. He was still treading on precarious ground and hoped to do better once he met the shah in person.

At long last Sultan Muhammad Shah was due to return to the city, and on June 8, 1334, the vizier ordered the visitors to ride out seven miles to meet the ruler. All brought gifts and were introduced to the sultan in a fixed order of precedence. Ibn Battuta had been rated a scholar and was so introduced.

The sultan took the traveler's hand and addressed him in Persian, "This is a blessing. Your arrival is blessed. Be at ease. I shall be compassionate to you and give you such favors that your fellow countrymen will hear of it and come and join you. Tell me, where are you from?"

"From the land of the Maghrib," replied Ibn Battuta, for so Morocco was known in that era.

They conversed for some minutes, and every time the sultan said anything encouraging Ibn Battuta kissed the royal hand until he had done so seven times. This again was a formula of which he had been apprised in advance. An apt and observant pupil, he was quick to follow customs of any country where he hoped for favors from royalty. He was rewarded by Muhammad Shah with a robe of honor, then withdrew.

A meal was served to all present, and on the following day each of the honored guests received a horse with rich trappings from the sultan's stable. The guests rode these mounts in the front of the procession when the sultan entered the city. It was a fabulous cavalcade, sixteen elephants with flags and gilded parasols leading the way for the monarch. On some of the elephants were military catapults charged with money. At intervals they bombarded gold and silver coins that the populace rushed to gather.

Riches flowed like water in this court. The next day Ibn Battuta was summoned to bring eight companions to the audience hall where great bags of money were brought in and distributed. The Moor received five thousand dinars. Another day he was assigned a stipend of twelve thousand dinars a year, and two more villages were added to the three whose revenues he had already been given. But still in this lavish court the Moor's debts haunted him. His creditors were clamoring for payment.

Word was sent among the visitors that anyone capable of being a vizier, secretary, military commander, judge, professor, or sheikh should make known his talents, and he would be appointed to that office. Many had come for the private reason that they wanted to gain quick riches and return to their countries, so most remained silent at first. Nevertheless the court officers were persistent.

"What do you say?" they asked Ibn Battuta.

"Vizierships and secretaryships are not my business," he replied, "but as to judges and sheikhs, that is my occupation and the occupation of my fathers before me."

Not knowing if he had given the right answer, Ibn Battuta awaited word from the palace. The message from the sultan arrived at a most awkward time when the Moor was unable to sit down properly because of a large boil on his posterior. However, one did not disregard a summons from royalty so Ibn Battuta presented himself at the room of the Thousand Pillars. When all were required to sit, Ibn Battuta, embarrassed, slipped away as unobtrusively as possible.

A second summons reached him, and one of the companions rose and in a low voice explained the traveler's absence. "He has a boil on the place where he sits."

There was a loud chuckle, and when Ibn Battuta joined the others at prayers in the audience hall, he saw them stifling covert smiles. Well, the boil was not on his knees, and he could still bend in the right direction to pray.

Now the sultan's decisions were to be announced. Three men were called one after the other and assigned posts in the realm, then the Moor went before the sultan, who was seated on a royal couch on a terrace, with the vizier and another official standing beside him.

Ibn Battuta made the customary obeisance to the sultan,

prostrating himself. Then the official announced formally, "Do homage, for the Master of the World has appointed you kadi of the royal city of Delhi and has fixed your stipend at twelve thousand dinars a year and assigned you villages to that amount of income and commanded for you twelve thousand dinars in cash, which you shall draw from the treasury tomorrow. He has given you a horse, saddle and bridle, and ordered you invested with a robe of honor."

The officer led Ibn Battuta before the sultan and presented him as the new judge.

"Do not think that this office of kadi of Delhi is one of the minor functions," the sultan admonished him in Persian. "It is the highest of functions in our estimation."

Though the Moor responded speaking Arabic, the two men understood each other and were able to converse.

"Will I be able to perform my duties adequately when I do not speak the language of the people?" Ibn Battuta asked.

"I have appointed two persons to aid you in that respect," the sultan told him. "You will be the one who signs all the legal documents. If," he added, "your stipend does not prove sufficient, I will give you the income from a hospice."

Ibn Battuta left the court pleased with his appointment, for he knew he was well qualified to interpret Muslim law. His long journey had brought material rewards. On the morrow he would pay his debts and after that he could live in comfort and experience the home life that had been lacking all these years. At the age of thirty he was willing to call a halt in his wanderings and make use of the learning he had acquired.

First there must be the reckoning with his creditors. It would require a large sum. Ibn Battuta had always been inclined to spend freely when he had funds at his command, and at this juncture his carefree financial management had caught up with him. Settlement of the accounts did not take place as promptly as he anticipated. Although he took up his duties at once, the promised payment did not reach him. He saw others receive sacks of money from the royal treasury, and he was counseled that all would be well—the sultan always kept his promises.

"Tomorrow" never came. Days, weeks, and months went by until half a year had passed. Debts for living expenses for his household piled up. Furthermore, the merchants who had financed him were about to set out for their own lands, and they were not willing to wait any longer.

Being desperate, but not wishing to anger the sultan, Ibn Battuta summoned his literary skill and wrote a long ode in praise of the ruler. Adroitly he inserted in it a line:

"I am in need, thy bounty's overflow."
and a little farther on he wrote:
"Make speed to aid the votary to thy shrine,
And pay his debt—the creditors are dunning."

Ibn Battuta delivered his ode to the sultan in person, placing it on his knee. Then he recited the lines aloud, asking the grand kadi to explain each.

The sultan liked Arabic poetry, as Ibn Battuta was aware, so he was delighted with the offering. When the recitation reached the part about making speed, he interrupted to say to the Moor, "I have compassion on you."

Ibn Battuta supposed that meant his strategy had been successful. He read his poem to the end and received congratulations from the courtiers. He was hoping for immediate action, but when nothing happened and a few more days passed, he wrote a formal petition requesting his promised stipend. He was notified that the debt was ordered paid, but still he saw no more money. The vizier went away from Delhi on other court matters, and the sultan absented himself on a hunting expedition.

What was Ibn Battuta to do? He was at the end of his resources, and his creditors left him no peace of mind. This was a sorry situation for a learned and respected judge. All those purchases at the frontier had brought no reward except promises. He had done everything to conform with the cus-

toms of the royal court, and what had been the result? He
was enmeshed in a financial tangle such as had never trou-
bled him when he was on the road traveling.

He decided upon drastic action. He had been told that
when money was lent to anyone under the sultan's protection
and royal payments that had been ordered were not made, it
was customary for the creditors to attack the debtor publicly.

Choosing a day when the sultan would visit his father's
grave, the Moor instructed the merchants, "When I go to the
palace, assail me for your debt according to the custom of the
country."

Ibn Battuta stationed himself at a vantage point where he
could see the sultan returning and said to his creditors, "This
is your moment."

Then he appeared as if he were about to enter the palace
gate. Out went the merchants shouting, "You shall not enter
until you have paid what you owe." They surrounded Ibn
Battuta, clamoring loudly.

The sultan was approaching and wanted to know the reason
for the hubbub. A clerk at the gate explained, and His Majesty
sent a doctor of law to ask details.

"He wishes to know the size of the debt," this official told
the merchants.

"Fifty-five thousand dinars," they chorused.

The sultan, who had by now entered the palace, sent out
word, "The sum will be paid, but the creditors' documents
must be verified."

The merchants presented their accounts, and the sultan
commanded that the proper amount of money be issued.

This was easier said than done, Ibn Battuta learned. The
official in charge of the treasury greedily demanded a bribe
of five hundred tangas before he would act. The Moor had
become money cautious through his expensive lesson. "Two
hundred," he offered.

The official refused to act. Once again the Moor was at a
dead end, which was awkward, for the sultan was about to

go on another hunt, and Ibn Battuta was supposed to accompany the party. He had already acquired a tent and arranged for men to carry him in a palanquin (an enclosed litter transported on the shoulders of four human bearers).

He was in no good mood when the expedition set out in great style with musicians, soldiers, guides, camels, and courtiers.

"The Moroccan is very upset," one of the sultan's friends told the ruler.

"Why so?"

"Because of his debt. His creditors are hounding him for payment."

The sultan expressed surprise, and the courtier explained, "Master of the World, you commanded the vizier to pay the kadi's debt, but the vizier left the city before this was done."

The sultan was thoughtful, for he had become attached to the Moor. "When we return to the capital," he told a member of the court, "go yourself to the treasury and see that this money is given to Ibn Battuta."

"O Master of the World," objected an envious official, "the Moroccan is very extravagant. I have seen him before this at the court of the Sultan Tarmashirin. Now he talks every day about the debt he has contracted."

Notwithstanding this criticism of the Moor's finances, the sultan invited Ibn Battuta to join him frequently. Once the ruler asked about the kinds of camels ridden to Mecca in the pilgrimage season, and the Moor told him about meharis (the elegant, fleet species of dromedary) and said he had one of this breed with him in Delhi. It required a special saddle, but an Egyptian Arab had made him a wax model of one, and Ibn Battuta had taken it to a carpenter who skillfully fashioned a duplicate. The Moor ordered it covered with blanket cloth and fitted with stirrups. On the day after his return from the hunt, he added a fine striped cloth and a silk bridle and prepared to send his camel to Muhammad Shah. Then he had a second inspiration, one last play he was going to make to win favorable action on his money problem.

In Ibn Battuta's party was a man from Yemen who was skilled in making candies. Although these had not pleased the Mongol sultan, there was a chance that Muhammad Shah had different tastes. Ibn Battuta had observed him devouring sweets.

Accordingly, the Moor requested the Yemenite to prepare a great quantity, shaped to resemble dates and other goodies. In all there were eleven plates and Ibn Battuta dispatched the entire lot to the sultan along with the camel. He also sent a gift to a courtier to persuade him to go to the sultan and say, "O Master of the World, I have seen a wonder. The Moroccan has sent a camel carrying a saddle."

"Bring it in," ordered the sultan.

A servant of the Moor led the animal into the sultan's tent, and he was delighted, for this was a present quite different from the multitude of gifts he was accustomed to receive. The servant mounted the saddle and walked the camel in front of Muhammad Shah, who rewarded him with two hundred dinars and a robe.

Taking heart, Ibn Battuta appeared in the public audience room with his eleven platters covered with silk napkins.

"What have you got in those plates?" the sultan inquired. "Surely it is sweetmeats."

"Yes, it is."

The ruler ordered the platters removed to his private sitting room, and there he lifted the covers and asked about the names of the confections. One kind, Ibn Battuta told him, was called judge's sweet mouthfuls.

"That is not true," declared a merchant who wished to humiliate the Moor. "This kind is called judge's sweet mouthfuls."

"You lie," another courtier spoke up, "and it is the kadi who speaks the truth."

"How so?" asked the sultan.

"O Master of the World, he is the judge, and these are his sweet mouthfuls, for he brought them."

"You are right," laughed the sultan.

He was in such good humor that he at last assumed a personal role in the settlement of Ibn Battuta's debts. At the end of the meal the treasurer approached the Moor and said, "Send your friends to receive the money."

Wondering what next would happen, Ibn Battuta returned to his house and found at last waiting for him three sacks of coins, enough to completely pay his debt and also the twelve thousand dinars the sultan had previously commanded. From this sum one tenth had been deducted, as was the custom of the court officers. A load was lifted from Ibn Battuta's conscience.

However, the entire experience had taught him a lesson. The sultan unfortunately was now aware of his financial weaknesses.

"Incur no more debts," Muhammad Shah told him a few days later, "and be not prodigal. Regulate your expenses according to what I have given you."

Ibn Battuta remembered Allah's admonition in the Koran: "Eat and drink but do not be too prodigious." He would watch his purse more closely after this, and he would have no more dealings with moneylenders.

IX
Lost Among the Infidels

When recalling his travels in later days, Ibn Battuta told little about his seven years in India. They were an interlude of luxurious court living, of expeditions in the sultan's train, of fitting up his house and building a mosque opposite it. Of his activities in jurisprudence we know nothing nor how he conducted his household. If he had any other children, he did not mention them. He truly felt the loss of the infant girl, whom he had adored. He went through a famine during which he dispensed food to the poor from a mausoleum foundation of which he had charge.

On another occasion the Moor accompanied the sultan on a campaign against a rebel governor and was present at a battle. On the return of the royal party to Delhi, Ibn Battuta fell into disfavor, not because he had again been profligate, but on account of his tendency to seek out holy men. He had visited a noted sheikh who had defied the sultan, refusing to take office under him. Later this man was executed after calling the sultan a traitor. At the time Ibn Battuta went to him, he was living in a cave outside Delhi.

When the sultan learned Ibn Battuta had been there, he gave orders that four of the royal slaves were to remain constantly with the Moor when he appeared in the audience hall. Ibn Battuta regarded this surveillance as a very bad sign and, fearing worse developments, fasted five days, tasted nothing but water, and read the Koran from cover to cover. He did not feel free of the sultan's intolerance until after the sheikh's death sentence was carried out.

This experience led him to withdraw from Muhammad Shāh's service, as he decided the contemplative religious life was more suited to his temperament than the opulent court of the ruler. He wearied of the constant danger of giving offense to his master, and all the while he pondered about finding a way to resume his travels. The promise he had given of remaining permanently in India no longer seemed binding since he had fallen from favor.

Outside the city lived a devout and humble imam known as the Cave Man, to whom Ibn Battuta attached himself as a follower. The holy man persuaded the Moor to give his possessions to the poor.

"I continued with him until the sultan sent for me and I became entangled in the world once again—may God give me a good ending!" Ibn Battuta related.

The sultan had been absent most of the time when the Moor was with the holy man, and hearing of his retreat, the ruler seems to have regretted the anger he had expressed toward Ibn Battuta. When the traveler answered the summons, he appeared in court clad as a mendicant.

"Will you not enter my service again?" the sultan asked in a most friendly manner.

Ibn Battuta declined with regret. "I would like permission to visit Mecca again," he said.

Muhammad Shah, professing to be a pious Muslim, could not refuse a request of that nature. So all was set early in December, 1341, for the Moor to depart on the pilgrimage as soon as the opportunity was presented. He may have devised this plan as the most plausible means of escape from the country without breaking his word. Ibn Battuta was always resourceful.

All circumstances seemed to favor the pilgrimage, and it is certain he was sincere about it, because he said afterward that when he exchanged the simple blue cotton tunic he wore while with the Cave Man for the robes of a gentleman once more, he could not bear to part with the garment. "Ever after, when I looked at it, I felt a light within me," he said.

The change in costume came unexpectedly and in a manner he could not refuse. Forty days after his conversation with the sultan, a royal messenger called upon the Moor, bringing saddled horses, slave girls and boys, a sum of money, and fine robes.

"The sultan commands your presence at court" was the word he brought. "He has an important commission for you."

Skeptical of the meaning of this order, Ibn Battuta nevertheless dressed in fitting attire and reported to Muhammad Shah.

The sultan was even more friendly than on their last encounter. "I have sent for you," he announced, "to go as my ambassador to the ruler of China, for I know your love of travel and sightseeing."

Nothing could have happened to furnish greater pleasure to Ibn Battuta. Again the predictions of the learned sheikhs in Egypt seemed likely of fulfillment; he regarded the forthcoming voyage as part of his destiny.

His was a peculiar errand. A delegation had arrived from China bearing a munificent gift and requesting that the sultan give permission to rebuild an idol temple in the Himalayas (thought by scholars to have been a site eighty miles east of Delhi) which the Muslim army had laid in ruins. Muhammad Shah was willing to give his consent, providing a poll tax was paid. He designated Ibn Battuta to deliver his reply, taking with him an even richer present than the sultan had received from China. The gift was to consist of one hundred thoroughbred horses, one hundred white slaves, one hundred Hindu dancing and singing girls, twelve hundred pieces of cloth, gold and silver candelabra and basins, brocade robes, caps, quivers, swords, pearl-embroidered gloves, and fifteen eunuchs. As one can judge from this list, slaves were common currency. Plenty were captured in the sultan's wars against the infidel inhabitants of India.

Ibn Battuta was to be accompanied by two other delegates, an emir and a eunuch who was a royal cupbearer. Another emir with a thousand horsemen would escort the party to the port of embarkation. With them went the fifteen Chinese ambassadors and their servants, about a hundred in all.

If the Moor expected a peaceful time of it, he was in for surprises. The expedition had not traveled a hundred miles when the military escort learned that Hindu infidels had surrounded a town seven miles off the route, so they went in that direction and fought a battle, resulting in great slaughter, because the enemy was taken completely by surprise. One of the few losses to the sultan's troops was the eunuch cupbearer. Word of his death was sent to Muhammad Shah, and the expedition waited to hear from him, as the eunuch had been in personal charge of the royal gift.

Meanwhile the infidel natives of India gave the party no respite. Raiders constantly swooped down on them from the hill country, and it became the habit of members of Ibn Battuta's escort to ride out daily with the military commander of the district to help him drive off the marauders.

One day Ibn Battuta with five friends went into a garden

to take their siesta, for this was in the hot season in August, 1342. They were wakened by the sound of shouting, and on riding toward a village to learn the cause, they ran into a host of attackers concealed in a thicket. There were too many to fight, so the group split up and fled. Ten of the assailants took out after Ibn Battuta, all but three giving up after a while. He had got into country where there was no road, and the ground was extremely stony. His horse's forefeet became wedged among the rocks, and he dismounted to free the animal.

The pursuers were still hot on his trail, so he mounted again, but soon his stirrup sword fell out of its scabbard. It was ornamented with gold, and he did not like to lose it, so he got down again, picked it up, and mounted once more. His flight looked hopeless until he came to a deep gully. He descended and led his horse into the tangle of bushes below. This was the last he saw of the men who were chasing him.

For the moment he was saved from the enemy, but he had no idea where he was. Working his way down the gully, he saw that it broadened ahead of him. There were tangled woods, but there was also a road. He was walking along it, not knowing where it led, when about forty Indians carrying bows emerged from the sheltering trees and surrounded him. He saw no other recourse but to throw himself on the ground and surrender, as he knew they would not kill a person who did so. The renegades stripped him of every article except his tunic, shirt, and trousers, and conducted him into the jungle to their camp near a water tank. They did not treat him badly, sharing with him a kind of bread made of peas and giving him water to drink. Two Muslims in their camp spoke Persian and asked who he was.

Ibn Battuta thought it wise to conceal his identity as the sultan's ambassador, so he gave only a partial answer, saying he had been a pilgrim to Mecca, that he was a traveler and a kadi.

The men who talked with him were sympathetic. "You are certain to be put to death either by the men we are with or by others who roam the country," one told him. The fellow indicated which was the leader, and Ibn Battuta said he would speak with him if the pair would act as interpreters.

The leader's only answer was to place the Moor in charge of an old man, his son, and an evil-looking black fellow, who, it was inferred, had been ordered to kill the prisoner. That evening the trio led him off to a cave, where they slept, the black with his feet on Ibn Battuta.

In the morning the Moor was convinced he had reached the end of his life. His captors took him back to the tank and made signs that they were going to finish the job and kill him.

Making an effort to be understood by signs and the few words he had picked up, Ibn Battuta pleaded with the old man, who seemed to harbor some pity for him. The Moor indicated that, by tearing off the sleeves of his shirt and giving them to the trio, it could be made to appear that he had escaped from them, and they would not be held to blame.

They remained aloof from this proposition, but took no steps to carry out their orders. About noon some newcomers arrived at the tank and urged the trio to join them and get their task finished. Instead, the old man and his companions refused and remained sitting on the ground around Ibn Battuta, with a hemp rope conveniently laid by.

"It is with this rope that they will bind me when they kill me," the Moor said to himself.

Pretty soon three members of the original party who had captured him came up and apparently asked, "Why have you not killed him?"

The old man pointed to the black, who by this time seemed to be sick. The old man was excusing the delay on that account.

Then, astonishingly, one of the newly arrived group, a pleasant-looking youth, addressed Ibn Battuta: "Do you wish me to set you at liberty?"

"Yes," the Moor answered fervently.

"Then go," the youth said. More than that, he accepted Ibn Battuta's tunic in exchange for a worn double-woven cloak he had brought and showed the Moor the way to get out of enemy country.

Fearing the men would change their minds and come after him, Ibn Battuta hid in a reed thicket, waiting until sunset and then walking until midnight in the direction the youth had pointed. He slept for a few hours near a hill and continued. Finding lotus trees growing on the way, he scratched his arms on the thorns while gathering the cherrylike fruit to eat.

He came out of the high land and reached a plain where there were cotton fields and castor-oil trees. At a well with a wall around it, he found a few mustard shoots floating in the water and was able to gather and eat some of them. He saved part for a later meal. He lay down to sleep under a tree, where fortunately he was not seen by a large party of mailed horsemen. While they rested at the well and washed their clothing, Ibn Battuta crept away into a cotton field and hid until night. When all was quiet in the camp, he set out in the moonlight, tramping until he arrived at a well under a dome. Here he ate the remaining mustard shoots and went to sleep inside the dome on a pile of grass.

He seemed to be getting no nearer to the region where he had become separated from the ambassadorial party, and from a position of affluence he was reduced to the lowly role of an indigent wayfarer whose life was constantly threatened. At least he was heartened by the belief that whatever happened was the will of Allah.

The road took him to a ruined village. The country round about appeared deserted, and he wondered that God, having preserved him this long, did not send someone to lead him to inhabited regions. Finally he saw cattle tracks and a sickle, then an infidel village which he avoided. At another place he found houses in ruins and, seeing two naked blacks, hid in fear. That night he entered the village and located a large grain storage jar with a hole in the bottom big enough to crawl into. He slept there, with a stone for a pillow. A bird perched on top of the jar kept fluttering its wings all night. "We were a pair of frightened creatures," Ibn Battuta related.

He wandered seven days before arriving at a village of unbelievers who had plots of vegetables and a water tank. When he asked for food, they refused him, but he found some radish leaves and ate them to appease his hunger. He had lost the urge to hide any longer, and when he learned infidel troops were in the village and a sentry challenged him, he simply sat down on the ground and did not answer. The man drew his sword and raised it to strike, but Ibn Battuta paid no attention he was so utterly weary. The sentry searched him, found nothing, and took the shirt with torn sleeves.

On the eighth day the Moor had been wandering without encountering water when he came to another ruined village that did not have the customary tank for gathering the drenching rains when they fell. An open, unwalled well was near the road, and a fiber rope was near it, but there was no vessel with which he could draw the precious liquid to drink. Always resourceful, Ibn Battuta tore a section from his turban cloth, tied it to the rope, and dropped it in the well. Drawing it up, he sucked the cloth. He dipped it repeatedly but he could not get enough moisture to satisfy his thirst, so he tied one of his shoes on the rope and brought it up full. It did not hold much, and he let it down again.

Alas, this time the end of the rope broke off and he lost the shoe. Well, one alone was no good, so he took the second shoe, tied it on, and this time drank until he was no longer thirsty.

Hesitant to walk completely barefooted through this rough country, Ibn Battuta tinkered with his remaining shoe, sliced the top off and tied the pieces on his feet with strips of torn cloth. In this way he had two soles on which to walk.

He was still at work tying knots when a black man appeared on the scene, carrying a jug and staff and with a wallet on his shoulder.

"Peace be with you," he said, giving the Muslim greeting.

At this welcome sound Ibn Battuta responded, "Upon you be peace and mercy and the blessings of God."

Speaking in Persian, the man asked, "Who are you?"

"A lost man."

"So am I, " said the stranger.

He tied his jug to the rope and brought up more water, then he opened the wallet and produced a handful of black chick-peas fried with rice and offered them to Ibn Battuta.

They ate together, sitting on the ground, made ablutions with water from the well, prostrated themselves toward Mecca, and prayed.

"What is your name?" the man asked.

"Muhammad," Ibn Battuta replied, giving his first name only. "What is yours?"

"Joyous Heart."

Ibn Battuta took this to be a good omen and began to hope that he would soon be out of his predicament.

"In the name of God accompany me," the man proposed.

This suited the Moor, but when they had gone only a little way his limbs gave out, probably as a result of his long period of hunger. He sat down.

"What is the matter?" the man wanted to know.

Ibn Battuta told him, "I was able to walk before meeting you, but now that I have met you, I cannot."

"Glory be to God!" the stranger exclaimed. "Then mount on my shoulders, and I will carry you."

"You haven't the strength for that," Ibn Battuta objected.

"No," the man replied, "perhaps not, but God will give me strength. You must do as I say."

The Moor allowed himself to be lifted up, and as the man set out, he counseled, "Keep saying, 'God is sufficient for us and an excellent guardian,' and I think that will help us along."

This is indeed a devout man, Ibn Battuta decided, and he repeated the words over and over again as they went along the road. He was so weary he could not keep his eyes open, and he fell asleep while riding on the man's shoulders. When he wakened, he was lying on the ground all alone near an inhabited village. Ibn Battuta entered it and learned it was a community of Hindu peasants in charge of a Muslim governor, so at last he was in safe surroundings.

The governor approached to investigate his presence, and they were able to converse. The Moor found he was not far from Koel, where the ambassadorial party had halted during the fighting. Soldiers, he was told, had come from there looking for him.

A horse was brought to carry Ibn Battuta to the governor's house, where he washed and was served a hot meal. The governor offered him a robe and a turban, saying, "These were left in my charge by an Arab from Egypt. He was one of the soldiers from the corps at Koel."

Ibn Battuta was surprised to find that they were two of his own garments, which he had exchanged with the Arab when they entered Koel. There was something mysterious about the whole episode of his being lost and found by the big black fellow. Then he remembered that the wise man of Alexandria had foretold, "You will enter the land of India and meet there my brother Dilshad, who will deliver you from a misfortune which will befall you then."

"Dilshad," he realized, was the Persian word for Joyous Heart.

The Moor felt he had been saved by a saint. Also one more of the prophecies had come true.

That night he wrote a note to Koel to inform his party of his safety. A messenger carried it to the city, and his companions brought clothing for him and a horse to carry him back to where the others waited. Word had been received from the sultan, they informed him, and he had sent another eunuch to replace the dead man. Orders were that the expedition must now continue on its way to China.

So once more Ibn Battuta would be on the high road to adventure. By the time he reached Koel he was completely recovered from his unfortunate experience. His companions interpreted what had happened to him and the eunuch as bad omens and wanted to return to Delhi, but the Moor was firm. They had orders from the sultan, and they must follow them.

X
To the Malabar Coast and the Maldive Islands

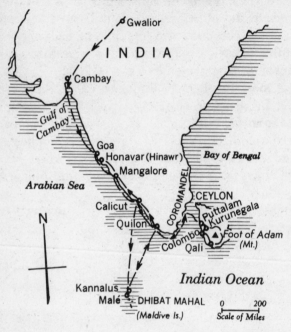

On the northern part of the coast of western India is a large indentation, the Gulf of Cambay, where Ibn Battuta's party reached the seacoast after a long trek. Sometimes they passed through infidel lands, other times through Muslim towns, and for a while in country where tigers prowled and preyed upon the population.

Cambay was then one of the principal seaports of India, and most of its inhabitants were foreign merchants. They had splendid mansions and mosques, and the harbor was full of boats that lay on the mud when the tide went out.

The expedition continued to Qandahar on the same gulf, and here the sultan welcomed them and offered the hospitality of his palace. A shipowner was expecting the ambassadors to embark at this point and held four vessels in readiness. The horses were divided among three of the boats, Ibn Battuta boarding the ship called *al-Jagir*, which carried seventy of the animals, fifty Abyssinian men-at-arms, and fifty rowers. The armed men were needed on the Indian Ocean to guarantee the safety of travelers against pirates and enemy raiders.

After five days' sailing the travelers arrived at Goa, and beyond that port they cruised along a coast where infidels allowed no Muslims inside their houses. When the vessels anchored at night, it was the custom to dispatch a gift to the ruler of the town, otherwise he would send a boat after them, and they would be doubly taxed.

The ships arrived at Mangalore, a great center of trade in spices, where pepper and ginger grew abundantly. After remaining three days they continued on the way to Calicut (present Kozhikode), far down toward the tip of India. This was one of the largest harbors Ibn Battuta had seen, visited by merchants from many lands, and it was the party's first destination, as here they were to board ships for China. They could not leave at once, for they must wait, as on the Yemen coast, for the season of the proper winds blowing consistently in one direction. Sailing with the monsoons was ever the rule on the Indian Ocean. Nowhere else in the world did the winds blow with such regularity at their different seasons.

Entering Calicut was a thrilling experience. Boats came out from shore to greet them with flags flying, drums beating, and trumpets and bugles blowing. Ibn Battuta was impressed by the sight of thirteen Chinese vessels anchored in the roadstead, mostly of greater size than the ships he was accustomed to seeing. Some had as many as twelve sails. The largest were called junks, the middle size ones were dhows, and the smallest were kakams.

Each member of the expedition was lodged in a house and told he would have to amuse himself for three months until the time of departure. Ibn Battuta passed this period learning what he could about the Malabar Coast and the customs of its infidel inhabitants. Although the sultan of Calicut was an infidel, he was used to dealing with foreigners in his port city and treated the visitors well.

A junk was assigned the ambassadors, and in the ensuing weeks Ibn Battuta discovered what he could expect of this mode of sea travel. A large ship might carry a thousand men, of whom six hundred were sailors and four hundred were warriors with bows, swords, and arbalests (crossbows) for hurling flaming naphtha at an enemy. Each large vessel was accompanied by three smaller ones to tow it in calm weather. The ships were built in Zaytun (present Tsinkiang, about three hundred miles northeast of Hong Kong) and Canton in China and were fitted with sails made of bamboo woven like mats. These were never lowered but were turned in the direction to catch the wind.

A junk might have four decks divided in cabins and salons for merchants. A cabin in turn had several chambers and a lavatory so that the occupant could take along his slave girls and wives. Sometimes on the long voyages, they remained all the time in these rooms without meeting other persons on shipboard until they got off at some port along the way. Sailors also had their families living on the ship, children too. They brought along wooden tubs to set on deck where they cultivated green vegetables and ginger.

The factor, who represented the shipowner, lived like a grand emir, going on shore preceded by archers and Abyssinians with their javelins, swords, drums, and bugles. Ibn Battuta was given to understand that the Chinese were the wealthiest people in the world, and viewing all these signs of pomp, he could well believe it.

He made the acquaintance of the factor with whom he was to travel and expressed his wishes: "I want a cabin to myself because of the slave girls, for it is my habit never to travel without them."

"The merchants from China," said the factor, "have taken all the cabins for the round trip. My son-in-law has a cabin which I can give you, but it has no lavatory. Perhaps you may be able to exchange it for another."

Ibn Battuta had to be satisfied with this arrangement, so he sent his companions and the slaves on board the Thursday before the ship was to sail. He would remain ashore for Friday prayers and join them afterward.

Friday morning his favorite slave boy returned ashore and told him the cabin was very small and unsuitable for so long a voyage.

Ibn Battuta sought out the captain at once and complained to him.

"It cannot be helped," the shipmaster said, "but if you would like to change to a kakam, there is one in which you may have cabins to suit you."

Ibn Battuta agreed and had his companions transfer his baggage and the slave girls to the smaller ship. All was in readiness before the hour of Friday prayer.

At this season every late afternoon at Calicut, the sea became stormy, and no one could embark until the water subsided. Almost all of the junks had departed ahead of the blow, and the only ones left in the harbor were a junk with the royal presents, the kakam on which Ibn Battuta was to travel, and another ship that was not going far.

It remained so stormy all the rest of Friday that Ibn Battuta, much against his wishes, had to spend the night ashore. He had nothing with him but a small rug on which he slept.

When he wakened and looked out to sea, the larger junk and the kakam had drifted far away, and there was bad news about the junk intended for the short voyage. The wind had blown it ashore, the vessel had broken up, and several aboard her had drowned.

The weather continued stormy. There was no means of joining the kakam, and the Moor spent an agonizing day worrying about how to get out to the boat. He was still ashore when night came on and with it another storm.

The second morning brought worse news. The big junk

carrying the sultan's present, the emir, and the eunuch who were to accompany Ibn Battuta had met the same fate as the earlier craft. The bodies of the two men who were to have gone with the Moor to China washed in on the beach, and Ibn Battuta had the unhappy task of supervising their burial. Crowds lined the shore seeking plunder cast up by the waves, and the sultan was on the beach directing his police to drive off the people and protect any treasure that floated in.

Meanwhile Ibn Battuta anxiously scanned the sea to find out how to join the kakam and his slaves. Eventually he saw the vessel vanish in the distance. Evidently the captain, aware of the fate that had overtaken the junks, decided to get out of Calicut Harbor without further delay.

There stood Ibn Battuta on the beach minus all his worldly goods. He had nothing left except ten dinars and the carpet he had slept on. Fate had handed him another blow. He had doubly failed in the assignment Sultan Muhammad Shah had given him, first getting lost and causing delay at Koel, then getting separated from his ship at Calicut. Even without the royal gift, he would have gone on to China to represent the ruler of India, but now what could he do?

One answer presented itself. He was informed that the kakam would put in at Quilon, another famous port near the tip of India, and he might overtake the vessel. The sultan of Calicut must have helped him with funds, for he was able to hire a boat on the inland waterway and horses for land travel the rest of the way of Quilon. It took ten days to reach there. Although he had been among infidels all of the way, Ibn Battuta found the city had a colony of Muslim merchants and a magnificent mosque. There was a Muslim hospice also, where he stayed and awaited news of the kakam. He heard nothing of it, but he did encounter the ambassadors of the emperor of China, who had been on another junk that was wrecked. Chinese merchants living in Calicut had provided them with clothes and arranged for their return to China.

When it appeared useless to wait any longer for word of the kakam, Ibn Battuta considered returning to Delhi and reporting to the sultan what had happened, but he feared the ruler would find fault with him for not remaining with the presents. At a loss as to the wisest course of action, he finally decided to go back to Calicut, and there he picked up a ride on a vessel bound for Honavar (Hinawr, just south of Goa), where on the journey he had met a most congenial Muslim sultan.

Ibn Battuta went directly to him and related the full story of his misadventures. This tactic had always proved the most efficient way out of his troubles, and he found now it was a partial solution. The sultan assigned him a lodging but no servant, and invited the Moor to recite prayers in his company. While he bided his time, Ibn Battuta spent many hours at the mosque and read the Koran daily. This diligence was invariably a sign that things were going badly with him.

Sultan Jamal ad-Din's attention was engaged in preparations for a foray against the ruler of Goa, whose son had quarreled with his father and invited the neighboring ruler to seize the town. The son pledged to accept Islam and marry the sultan's daughter. The sultan was about to sail for Goa with fifty-two vessels.

Ibn Battuta did not know whether he ought to disassociate himself from this fracas. Usually he could find an answer to any dilemma in the holy book, so he opened the Koran to take an augury. At the top of the page he read: "In them is the name of God frequently mentioned, and verily God will aid those who aid Him."

Taking it that this related to the conversion of the son to Islam, Ibn Battuta approached Sultan Jamal ad-Din following afternoon prayer and said, "I wish to join the expedition."

"In that case you will be their commander," exclaimed the sultan, delighted to hear of the augury.

The inhabitants of Goa were prepared for battle and had set up mangonels (stone- and missile-throwing engines) for defense of the city. Jamal ad-Din's fleet arrived Monday night and advanced toward shore Tuesday morning, the Muslim army jumping into the water, shields and swords in hand. Ibn Battuta jumped in with them. It was the first time he had ever been in the midst of a battle, but it was a victory from the start. The sultan at once took possession of the palace and gave adjacent houses to his courtiers.

The Moor remained three months in Goa, then went back to Honavar. He was now in good standing and moved around the country, going again to Calicut and to the neighboring town of Chale (Beypore), famed for the beautiful fabrics manufactured there. When Ibn Battuta returned to Calicut, he encountered two of his slaves who had been on the kakam. They had come from the islands to the east, and they told him the king of Sumatra had taken the Moor's slave girls, his goods had been seized, and his companions were scattered far and wide.

On going back to Honavar, Ibn Battuta learned there had been an uprising at Goa against its recent conqueror. The revolt was led by the former ruler, and the Muslim troops were in a state of siege. The Moor did not wish to get involved again in battle, so he made up his mind to travel to the Maldive Islands, lying off the southwest tip of India. The people there had been converted to Islam in the twelfth century, and although other travelers had spoken of visiting the archipelago, nothing had ever been written of it.

It was easy for Ibn Battuta to find a boat at Calicut going in that direction. He was ten days sailing to the islands, which were mostly grouped in circular clusters, each with a single entrance for vessels. The Moor was told there were about two thousand islands in all. He was not aware that they were actually seventeen huge coral atolls, and this was why they were close together, with the tops of palm trees on one visible from others. They were divided into twelve districts, each under a governor, with the sultan residing on Malé.

Ibn Battuta went ashore at Kannalus, where there were many mosques, and he easily found lodging in the home of a pious Muslim. The main food of the islanders, he learned, was a red-fleshed fish like bonito, which when smoked was tasty enough to export in quantities. The other staple food was the coconut, that product which had so astounded Ibn Battuta when he traveled the western shore of the Indian Ocean. As for grains, the islanders grew only a cereal resembling millet. They were extremely self-sufficient, industrious, and not given to fighting. Ibn Battuta observed, "Their armor is prayer."

He found the Maldivians very cleanly and inclined to perfume themselves with scented oils such as sandalwood. Their garments were almost too simple for his sophisticated tastes, as they wore only a kind of apron tied around their waists in place of trousers and another cloth over their backs. Their headgear was either a turban or a small kerchief. All persons of high or low order went barefoot, and for this reason on entering a house they always washed their feet with water from a jar kept in the vestibule and wiped them on palm matting. They did this also on going into a mosque. Their money consisted of cowrie shells gathered from the sea. With these shells they trade for rice from Bengal and for products of the Yemenites. The cowries were readily accepted as money in the countries having commerce with the islands, and Ibn Battuta saw them exchanged at the rate of 1,150 for a gold dinar.

When Ibn Battuta had spent two weeks at Kannalus, he embarked on a ship bound for Coromandel (the east coast of India, as the Malabar is the west coast) and other places to the east, from which he intended to obtain passage to China. He wished to visit the mosque at Malé on the way. However, he had met a man from India, who warned him that, if he went ashore on the island of Malé, the vizier was sure to detain the Moor, as his kadi, for the capital city lacked a properly trained judge. For this reason Ibn Battuta was extremely cautious about landing. He requested the captain of the boat to say, if anyone inquired for him, that he did not know of any such passenger. He had no intention of remaining in the islands, no matter what post was offered him. However, although Ibn Battuta was unaware of it, someone had already written from Kannalus informing the vizier that the former kadi of Delhi was in the Maldives.

Ibn Battuta enjoyed his voyage among the atolls, he and his companions being hospitably entertained wherever the boat stopped. On the tenth day he reached Malé and unobtrusively stepped ashore, bound for the mosque to say his prayers. He had no sooner done so than an officer stopped him and said he must first call upon the vizier, whose name was Suleiman.

Ibn Battuta was dismayed, for the ship he was on would have taken him a considerable distance on his way to China, which it was now his firm intention to visit. The captain kept his word, and when they went to the palace, he said he knew nothing about any kadi from Delhi.

Nevertheless, the vizier insisted upon providing lodging for Ibn Battuta, sending him platters of rice, salted meat, chickens, butter, fish, and all the conceivable foods his party would need, also a robe and 100,000 cowries for expenses. It was clearly impossible for the Moor to depart with his boat. It went on without him, for he could see no avenue of escape from this enforced hospitality. Ten days later a ship came in from Ceylon with some Arab and Persian dervishes aboard. They recognized Ibn Battuta and confirmed to the vizier that he was a well-known kadi, so the pretense of his only being a Muslim traveler had to end, and the Moor was forced to resign himself to an indefinite residence in the Maldives.

Before the visiting dervishes departed, Ibn Battuta asked permission to give a banquet in their honor, to which he invited some of the high court officials. The vizier brought an elevated pavilion on which to be seated. Emirs and ministers surrounded him. They all threw down lengths of cloth as gifts for the dervishes.

These holy men put on a strange performance for the gathering, having requested Ibn Battuta to prepare a bed of hot coals in the garden of his house. After chanting and ritual dancing, the dervishes walked barefoot on the coals, and some picked up the hot charcoal and ate it as though it were candy.

The vizier remained throughout this performance, and Ibn Battuta accompanied him on the walk to the palace. As they passed an orchard belonging to the royal treasury, the vizier said, "This orchard is yours, and I shall build a house for you to live in."

What could Ibn Battuta do? There was no way out. In spite of the islanders' goodwill, the Moor was being very firmly held captive.

A day or so later the vizier sent two slave girls, pieces of silk, and a casket of jewels to his unwilling guest. This led to a proposal that Ibn Battuta should marry the vizier's daughter.

The Koran permitted a Muslim man four wives and as many other women for concubines as he wished. Ibn Battuta had had his share of female companions the past ten years, but he was not a family man, and if there were any women in his life whom he regretted losing, he never mentioned them. Women did not rank high in the Arab lands, and he was confounded by the fact that the Maldives were ruled by a sultana.

Her name was Khadija, and she had inherited sovereignty from her grandfather, father, and minor brother. None of the royal house survived except Khadija and her two younger sisters. She had married the Sheikh Jamal, who had helped bring up the royal children, and he therefore merited the title of vizier, so there were two men of this high rank on the island. Jamal was the real holder of authority, though orders were issued in his wife's name only. To this man it became necessary for Ibn Battuta to ask permission to accept the Vizier Suleiman's proposal. A messenger was sent to the palace, and he returned to the Moor with the unexpected statement that the request was denied. The reason given was that Jamal wished Ibn Battuta to marry his own daughter as soon as her period of mourning for her recently deceased husband came to an end.

There was no sentiment in this bargaining for unseen wives, but Ibn Battuta did not wish to wed Jamal's daughter. He thought she brought ill luck. She had already had two husbands, both of whom had died before they consummated the marriage. About this time the Moor became sick with a fever that was common in the islands, and he decided to get out of his entanglements by secretly hiring a boat to take him to Bengal, on the mainland. To pay his way he sold some of the jewels that had been given him.

But the Vizier Suleiman heard of his plan and refused to consent to his departure unless the Moor returned all that had been given to him. He wanted the gold returned—not cowries. Ibn Battuta was in a bind, for the vizier had craftily forbidden the town merchants to help solve his financial problems. Once more money matters had entrapped the Moor, and when it was clear that it was impossible for him to get out of the islands, Sheikh Jamal, the sultana's husband, sent a courier to say, "Stay with us and you shall have what you will."

Ibn Battuta reasoned that, if he did not remain of his own free will, he would be detained anyhow, so it was better to agree. He thereupon called on Jamal and told him, "If you wish me to stay, I have some conditions to make."

One was that he did not wish to walk in the streets on foot, so he was given a mare. Only royalty rode in the islands, and when Ibn Battuta appeared on a horse, he was followed by inquisitive men and boys. The vizier stopped that by sending a crier through the town beating a brass plate and proclaiming that Ibn Battuta was to be left alone.

The Moor's financial affairs were also adjusted, and the matter of his first proposal of marriage with Suleiman's daughter was resumed, the sultana's husband giving consent. A feast was arranged at the royal palace, and all was in readiness for the ceremony when the bride refused to attend. Suleiman said she was sick.

In another time and place this would have been a comical situation. But with the two viziers of the Maldive Islands, it was a serious transaction. Vizier Jamal privately whispered to Ibn Battuta regarding Suleiman's daughter, "She has refused, and she is her own mistress. The people have assembled for the ceremony, so what do you say to marrying the sultana's mother-in-law?"

"Very well," the Moor agreed. Naturally he was not acquainted with either of these women.

A kadi and notaries attended to the formalities. The profession of faith was recited, the vizier paid the lady's dowry, and the wedding was over. The bride was conducted to Ibn Battuta a few days later.

This sight-unseen marriage was not as bad an arrangement as might have been expected. Ibn Battuta said afterward of the bride, "She was one of the best of women." He was no longer a young man, and he seems to have found this older wife comfortable to live with.

He resigned himself to becoming kadi, partly as penalty for having criticized his predecessor for charging too heavy a toll upon estates for his fees and for "never having done anything properly."

Ibn Battuta was determined all procedures should be carried out according to sacred law. For instance, he stopped the custom of divorced wives remaining in the houses of their former husbands and had about twenty-five men punished for countenancing this. He also made strict rules about attendance at Friday services. Any man not appearing at the mosque would be beaten and paraded in the bazaars. The Moor saw to it that the muezzins and prayer leaders were assiduous in their duties. He tried to enforce an order that women wear more clothing (he had been shocked in the islands to see them going about bare from the waist up). When he was unable to change this custom, he insisted that at least no woman be admitted to his presence in a lawsuit unless her body was covered.

In the months that followed Ibn Battuta took his full quota of wives, marrying three more from families high in the realm. One was the granddaughter of a former sultan, and another had been the wife of the previous sultan, who had been deposed. The Moor's access to royal circles roused considerable animosity as did also his severe interpretations of law, and finally Jamal summoned him in a rage.

Ibn Battuta omitted his usual obeisance to the vizier and merely saluted him with a "Salaam Alaykum" ("Peace be with you"). Then, turning to the courtiers gathered around, he declared, "Be my witnesses that I resign the office of kadi because of my inability to carry out its duties."

Vizier Jamal voiced his complaints, to which Ibn Battuta replied in the most uncompromising manner. At this point the muezzin chanted the call to sunset prayer, and Jamal had to cut short his argument. He went to the palace, muttering, "They say I am sultan, but I sent for this fellow to vent my wrath on him, and he vented his wrath on me."

Ibn Battuta well knew that he had a certain invulnerability, because he had been honored and employed in the service of the sultan of India. Though the islands were far from Delhi, there was fear in this remote capital of powerful Muhammad Shah's disapproval.

Jamal decided to restore the earlier kadi to his post and to permit Ibn Battuta to continue on his way. An order arrived from the palace stating, "You are aiming only to leave us. Give back your wives' dowries and pay your debts and go, if you will."

Ibn Battuta acted at once and paid off his accounts, but

before he could leave, the vizier had already changed his mind and withheld permission for his departure. Ibn Battuta swore a solemn oath that he had no recourse but to go. He removed his possessions to a mosque on the seashore and brooded on some rebellious thoughts about island rule. With two ministers he plotted to go to a place on the Coromandel coast, where the ruler was husband of the Moor's favorite wife's sister, and fetch troops to conquer the islands. The ministers proposed that then Ibn Battuta should be placed in charge as the ruler's representative.

The Moor and the two ministers worked out details of the revolt, such as hoisting a white flag on shore when all was in readiness for the invasion. However, Jamals' suspicions were aroused, and instead of trying to delay the Moor, he now wished to hasten his departure. Ibn Battuta took off for one of the other islands, but no sooner had he done so than his favorite elder wife became ill and wished to go back. Ibn Battuta reluctantly divorced her and left her to make arrangements to return to Malé while he went on to join a ship bound for the Coromandel coast. There were more delays, but finally he got away from the Maldives on August 22, 1344. It had been nineteen years since he left his home in Tangier.

He would remember the tropical archipelago for the women who had been part of his existence there. Many a man has dreamed of a life of luxury beneath the palms, replete with a harem. Ibn Battuta had all of that and was happy to leave it. He still had a wandering foot.

XI

From Ceylon by Junk to China

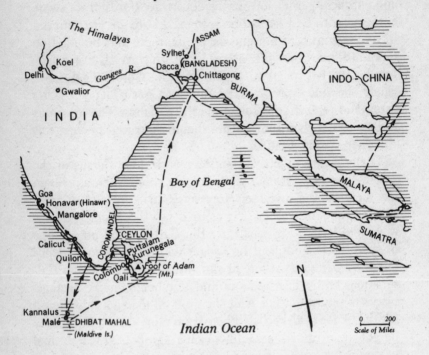

Off the southeast tip of India lies Ceylon with its striking mountain, Adam's Peak, which Muslims believed bore the footprint of the first man. (Buddhists venerated it as the footstep of Buddha, and Brahmans believed Siva left his mark there.)

Ibn Battuta gazed at the island's low coast, fringed with coconut palms, and counted upon being put ashore at the first port the ship approached. Instead, the crew sailed by, declaring that the sultan of that place was evil and encouraged pirates to operate out of his harbor.

A gale had arisen, and the boat was in danger. Ibn Battuta, with his recurrent fear of stormy seas, insisted, "Put me ashore, and I shall get you a safe conduct from this sultan."

The captain sent him to land in a small craft, and when Sinhalese (the people of Ceylon) came out and demanded who he was, the Moor replied, "I am a friend of the brother-in-law of the sultan of Coromandel. I am on my way to visit him, and the contents of the ship out there are a present for him."

The men told him they would have to notify the sultan at Puttalam (a town in western Ceylon). Ibn Battuta waited until he was sent for by the ruler. He was again in spice country, traveling to the capital through a land of cinnamon trees. His report is among the first historical mentions of them. He found Puttalam a small, pretty town surrounded by wooden walls with wooden towers.

The infidel sultan could speak Persian and appeared delighted with the stranger. He told Ibn Battuta his companions might land in safety because he was on good terms with the sultan of Coromandel. The Moor remained three days, spending much time in the company of the ruler, who liked to hear tales his guest told of rulers and other countries. There were pearl fisheries off the island, and the sultan presented Ibn Battuta with some valuable specimens of the jewels, saying, "Do not be shy about receiving them. Ask me for anything you want."

"Since arriving in Ceylon," the Moor replied, "I have had but one desire, to visit the blessed Foot of Adam."

"That is readily accomplished," said the ruler. "I shall send a party to escort you to it."

The sultan gave Ibn Battuta a palanquin carried by slaves and sent with him four yogis (Hindu ascetics) whose custom it was to make an annual pilgrimage to the top of the peak. Three Brahmans, ten other persons, and fifteen men to carry provisions went along.

Although the 7,352-foot mountain had been plainly visible from the coast, getting to its summit meant a considerable journey. The expedition camped the first night by a river and crossed it in the morning on a bamboo raft. That day they reached the last town in the sultan's territory, and a feast was prepared for them. Next they entered rugged country where Ibn Battuta saw many elephants. They arrived at Kurunegala, the capital of another sultan, near the Lake of Rubies, where many precious stones were found. The sultan of this place owned a white elephant, and when he rode it in festivals, he adorned its forehead with great rubies.

Ibn Battuta discovered that he was in the midst of marvelous gem country, where men dug for rubies, sapphires, and topazes. Those of great value belonged to the sultan, who paid a price for them, but the diggers could keep the lesser jewels.

The party continued southeast from Kurunegala to the Lake of Monkeys, and Ibn Battuta saw some of the animals, black, with long tails and bearded like men. He was told they had a king of their own and that he wore a crown of leaves.

The travelers left the inhabited country behind, passed some grottoes, and began their climb through heavy vegetation. As they mounted the steep slope, the clouds closed in below, shutting off a view of the base. Two paths led upward, the Baba, or Father, trail being more difficult. A stairway had long ago been cut in the rock, and at ten different places along the route, iron stanchions and chains had been installed for climbers to hold on to in pulling themselves up.

From the last chain to the grotto of Khidr was seven miles. Here pilgrims left their belongings and ascended two more miles to the blessed footprint of Father Adam on a lofty black rock. (It was a depression measuring 5 feet 4 inches by 2 feet 6 inches in size.) Holes had been cut in this stone where infidel pilgrims placed offerings of gold and precious gems. Dervishes watched for these gifts and raced each other to garner them as soon as visitors had gone.

It was the custom to remain three days at the grotto of Khidr and visit the footprint every morning and evening, so Ibn Battuta did this and then went off the mountain by way of the Mamma track, stopping at villages on the way. He swung around the south side of the mountain, visiting Colombo (modern capital of Ceylon), then went back to Puttalam, where his ship captain was waiting. The Moor thanked the sultan for his cooperation in providing an escort and making it so easy for him to visit the holy spot. Then the boat sailed for the Coromandel coast, his earlier destination.

This was not to be the uneventful three-day journey Ibn Battuta anticipated. As they neared the coast, a high wind sprang up, and the boat ran aground in shallow water six miles from shore. There was near panic on board, some thinking their last day had arrived. The sailors put together a raft, but it would not carry everyone. Ibn Battuta sent two slave girls with it—there was room for only one, but the other, who was a good swimmer, hung on to the ropes. Both reached shore safely. Ibn Battuta sent his most valued possessions with them —his jewels and store of ambergris, a commodity much valued in this part of the world. He prepared to take a chance on being rescued. God would look out for him, he felt certain.

Almost everyone had left the stranded vessel on makeshift rafts when in the morning a party of infidels came out in a boat and took Ibn Battuta and the remaining men ashore. The Moor explained that he was a relative of the sultan, so a message was sent to the ruler, who was absent in the country. On shore Ibn Battuta was reunited with his companions and his slave girls and the captain of the boat. After a wait of three days word arrived from the sultan, instructing the Moor to join him. A palanquin and ten horses were provided for his convenience, and when he arrived at the sultan's camp, he was given a cordial reception. Ibn Battuta discussed with his relative by marriage the matter of sending an army to subdue the Maldive Islands, a scheme which met with the sultan's approval. However, he pointed out, the winds were against taking immediate action, as it would be three months before the monsoons permitted boats to be sailed in that direction.

While waiting, Ibn Battuta journeyed inland to the capital but found it plague ridden. The sultan's family were sick; the sultan himself became ill and died within a fortnight. His nephew succeeded him, and this altered the plan for conquering the islands. The Moor caught the fever too and was so sick he thought his time had come. He dosed himself with tamarind and recovered, but was in a mood where he'd had enough of Coromandel. Though the new sultan promised that within a month the expedition could leave for the Maldives and that the Moor would be suitably rewarded if they were subdued, Ibn Battuta refused to go along. In that case, the new sultan said, the Moor might leave on any ship he chose.

He returned to the port and found there some vessels bound for the Yemen, so he embarked in one and went as far as Quilon on the west side of the tip of India. He intended to go back to Honavar, where he had been so well treated by the ruler, but when nearly there a dozen infidel ships came out and attacked the vessel, robbing everybody on board. They stripped Ibn Battuta of his jewels, clothes, and traveling provisions, leaving him nothing but his trousers. The boat was taken, and the men on it were put ashore. Ibn Battuta, feeling extremely abashed in such reduced circumstances, made his way to Kozhikode (Calicut) and to a mosque, where with true Muslim generosity one of the theologians supplied him with a robe, the kadi sent a turban, and a merchant provided another robe.

He did not say how he managed to raise funds to return to the Maldive Islands, but he had learned that the Sultana Khadija had remarried, so a new vizier was in charge there. Ibn Battuta had been told that a wife he had left behind had given birth to a son. From Kannalus he sent word to the vizier that he had come to fetch his boy. The mother objected.

When Ibn Battuta reached Malé, he thought better of the matter. He saw the little boy, but after all, how was a restless traveler like himself to make provision for a small child on his journeys? It would be better to resume his long-delayed voyage to China. Therefore he agreed that the little boy should remain with his mother. When he asked the vizier's permission to depart, the latter generously furnished him with robes and cowries for the trip.

Forty-three days later Ibn Battuta arrived far up the northeast coast of what is now Bangladesh. It is thought he landed at Chittagong. This was one spot where the Moor avoided visiting the sultan, who, he understood, was an enemy of Muhammad Shah. It would not therefore be wise for the Indian ruler's ambassador to China to present himself to the monarch. If it seems presumptuous for Ibn Battuta to regard himself as still ambassador, after having been stripped of his possessions and spending so long getting this far on the way, it can only be said he refused to give up his purpose.

He had a reason for stopping in Bangladesh. He wished to reach Assam in the Himalayas foothills in order to call upon a noted Muslim saint who was living there, a sheikh originally from Tabriz. This man had psychic powers, and two days before Ibn Battuta reached his destination, four of the sheikh's followers came out to greet the Moor, saying they had been ordered by the holy man to welcome the traveler from the West.

He found the sheikh had established a hermitage outside a cave and had converted many of the mountain people to Islam. Ibn Battuta remained three days at this place and during his visit admired a wide mohair mantle the sheikh was wearing. When it came time to say good-bye, his host took off the garment and gave it to him. On the way out dervishes told Ibn Battuta, "The sheikh was not in the habit of wearing that mantle, but put it on purposely. He said when he did so, 'This will be asked for by the Moroccan, and it will be

141

taken from him by an infidel sultan, who will give it to our brother Burhan ad-Din, whose it is and for whom it was made.' "

Ibn Battuta objected to this statement. He assured the dervishes, "This mantle represents to me the sheikh's blessing, and I will not enter the presence of any sultan, infidel or Muslim, while wearing it."

The Moor made his way to the Blue River, or Meghna (an eastern tributary of the Ganges), and traveled down it fifteen days, finding the country resembled the Nile Valley, with waterwheels, orchards, and villages. At a port fifteen miles southeast of Dacca a junk was on the point of sailing for Sumatra, so he embarked on it.

The first stop was on the Burma coast two weeks later. The sultan of the place came riding out on an elephant, on which was mounted a kind of packsaddle made of skins. Ibn Battuta regarded the inhabitants of this land with curiosity. The women impressed him as beautiful, but the men, though of stature like other humans, had mouths which to him appeared like those of dogs. These men went naked except for an ornamental pouch of woven reeds suspended from their waists. The women wore aprons made of leaves of trees. The Moor, unaccustomed to so much nudity, declared they were a savage rabble living very simply in grass and reed huts on the seashore. Elephants furnished the prevailing mode of transport.

The sultan was scarcely less barbaric than his people. He was dressed in goatskins with the hair outside and wore on his head three bands of colored silk. He carried a javelin, which must have been of bamboo, and was accompanied by twenty men riding elephants. It was his custom to exact tribute from every ship that put in at his port, requiring payment of a slave girl, a white slave, gold ornaments, and enough cloth to cover an elephant.

The captain of the junk appears to have bypassed this tribute and sent instead a present of spices, cured fish, and Bengali cloth. It was said that, if anyone failed to meet the sultan's demands, he would put a spell on the ship, raise a storm at sea, and cause all or nearly all to perish. If any such curse was put upon Ibn Battuta's junk, it was in vain, for the ship arrived safely twenty-five days later at Sumatra and coasted along the verdant shore of the island to a large village, where Ibn Battuta landed. He found another form of wealth in this place. The merchants carried on trade with pieces of tin and unsmelted chunks of Chinese gold.

Arab traders had reached Sumatra, and Ibn Battuta had little difficulty in communicating. A representative of the local admiral, who had given permission for merchants and others to land from the junk, sent a letter to the sultan informing him of the Moor's status and that he was a noted Muslim traveler. Shortly thereafter an emir, a kadi, and several doctors of law put in an appearance, bringing horses for Ibn Battuta and his companions to ride to the capital.

In this strange tropical island he knew not what to expect. Would it be like India or have customs all its own? With the riders he entered a wooden-walled city and proceeded to a place where spears were stuck in the ground on both sides of the road. Here everyone was told to dismount and go on foot the rest of the way. They walked to an audience hall and were greeted by the sultan's lieutenant, who then wrote a note to the sultan, sealed it, and gave it to a page. The party waited until he brought back a written reply. Then another page appeared, carrying a linen bag.

The lieutenant took Ibn Battuta by the hand and led him into a small house, opened the bag, and brought out three aprons. One was of pure silk, another of silk and cotton, and the third of silk and linen. The Moor regarded them perplexedly. These were undergarments, he was informed, and here were three called middle clothing, three woolen mantles, and three turbans. Ibn Battuta was to select one of each and

143

put them on, employing the apron of his choice in place of trousers. The companions would do the same with the rest of the garments. Ibn Battuta remembered the time on the African coast when he had been obliged to don wraparound clothing instead of trousers. Amiably he put on the gift attire, ate lunch, and rode with the lieutenant to a garden surrounded by a wooden wall. Here, at a little house carpeted with strips of cotton velvet, two slave girls and two servants were brought in and given to Ibn Battuta in behalf of the sultan. The guest was told it was the custom for a newcomer to wait three nights before saluting the ruler. The visitors would remain at this place in the meantime. Food was sent in thrice daily, and fruits and sweetmeats morning and evening.

On the fourth day, which was Friday, the emir said, "You will salute the sultan today in the royal enclosure of the cathedral mosque after the service."

Wearing his unaccustomed island garments, Ibn Battuta introduced himself to the ruler, who shook his hand and invited him to sit down and tell all about Sultan Muhammad Shah and what else he had seen on his travels. Quite at home in this role, the Moor narrated a sampling of his adventures, selected from his very ample repertoire. Later in the day the sultan changed the robes he had worn in the mosque for royal robes and rode away from the building on a richly caparisoned elephant, his suite accompanying him on horses. Ibn Battuta went along with them to the audience hall, again dismounting where the lances were placed in the ground.

The sultan remained seated on his elephant in the hall, where male musicians were brought in to play for dancing horses that wore golden anklets and embroidered silk halters. The sight of the pirouetting animals fascinated Ibn Batttuta, though he had seen something similar at the court in Delhi.

For fifteen days the traveler enjoyed the hospitality of the Sumatran monarch, then he requested permission to continue his journey, since the winds were blowing in the right direction for China. A junk was located on which he could depart for that land, and the ruler outfitted it with comforts, provisions for the travelers, and rich presents.

Ibn Battuta's luck was with him once more. He felt that he was actually on his way to his long anticipated destination. The ship sailed twenty-one days along the coast of the Malay Peninsula, arriving at an infidel land which may have been near the Kelantan River on the northeast frontier of present Malaysia. At one port a number of junks were assembled, ready to make piratical raids. The Moor and his fellow travelers went ashore and observed that elephants were more numerous than ever and were used by the people to carry loads. Each shopkeeper had his elephant picketed near by.

The infidel sultan heard about Ibn Battuta and summoned him to his place of audience, though they had no common language in which to speak. The natives understood only part of the Moor's greeting, the word *as-salaam*, "peace." A square of cloth was ordered spread for him to sit on, though the sultan himself sat on the ground. Someone explained that the cloth was to show the visitor honor. An interpreter having been found, the sultan asked about the ruler of Delhi, then said, "You shall be our guest three days, and after that you may go."

While the audience continued, Ibn Battuta saw a man approach with a hooked knife. He delivered a long speech, completely incomprehensible to the Moor. Then, before the latter's horrified eyes, the man gripped the knife with both hands and cut his own throat. The blade was so sharp his head fell to the ground.

Ibn Battuta started back in horror at the sight of the bleeding body at his feet.

Observing this, the sultan inquired curiously, "Doesn't anyone do this in your country?"

"I have never seen such a thing," the shaken Moor replied.

"These are our slaves," laughed the sultan. "They kill themselves for love of us."

It was explained that the man's speech had been a declaration of affection for the sultan. He had said his father had done the same thing and so had his grandfather.

The sultan gave orders to carry the body away and cremate it. Ibn Battuta understood a large pension would be assigned to the children, widow, and brothers of the dead man.

Again the Moor boarded the ship, and it sailed for thirty-four days before arriving at the sluggish, red-tinged waters of a portion of the China Sea. Because here the ocean had no waves or movement, this was where the large junks needed to be taken in tow and rowed by three of the smaller ones. In addition to the tugging of these vessels, the large one carried twenty huge oars and was rowed by two rows of men standing up facing each other and chanting in musical voices as they pulled on thick cables attached to the oars.

It took thirty-seven days to cover this monotonous stretch of water. The sailors considered it a fast crossing. Usually forty days were required.

Since this part of the route is not clearly defined, no one is sure in what country Ibn Battuta next landed. He called it Tawalisi and said its people looked somewhat Turkish. Wherever he stopped, he was only an additional seventeen days at sea before arriving at China, the farthest land he was destined to visit. He had spanned nearly half the globe.

XII
The Terrifying Land of the Mongol Khans

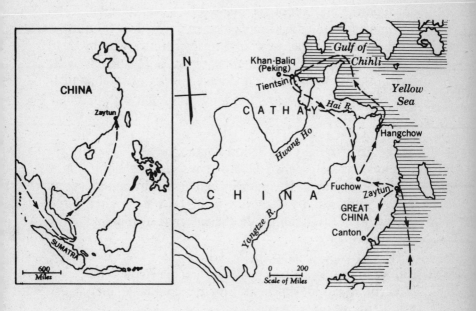

Ibn Battuta was by this time forty-one years old, a man of the world with more experiences behind him than a score of average persons might have had during their entire lives. He had depended upon his wits to carry him from one far side of the known world to the other far side. He traveled in style to China, but how he accomplished this feat will never be completely known, nor can his exact itinerary after he arrived there be traced.

In this distant land there were still Muslims to greet him and invite him to their quarters in each large Chinese city. There were still mosques for the Friday services.

As far back as A.D. 700 Arab merchants had visited Chinese ports. Muslims for centuries had dominated the oriental trade routes, and Persian mixed with Arabic and local terminology became the lingua franca (common language) of commerce on the China coast. The dialect had been learned from merchants and spread by sailors. Chinese aristocrats looked down on the business of trading and therefore tolerated Muslim colonies in their maritime cities, who would carry on trade for them. Place names were known largely to travelers by their Persian versions, and there were direct ship contacts with India, Arabia, and Persia. Thus amid the vast oriental population of this unknown land, the Moor was aware he could find little islands of Islam where he would be understood and helped on his way.

The first city he reached was Zaytun (present Tsinkiang), an immense metropolis where damask silk and satin fabrics were manufactured. He guessed the port might be the largest in the world. In its harbor were at least a hundred large junks, and he saw a multitude of small craft such as had never met his eyes before.

He had gone farther up the China coast than most later European travelers did. Vessels in the pepper trade unloaded at Zaytun's harbor, which was situated on a large inlet of the sea.

On the day Ibn Battuta stepped ashore, he saw the Chinese emir who had gone to India carrying presents to the sultan and who had afterward set out from Delhi with the ambassadorial party. This man had been shipwrecked on one of the junks at Calicut, and Ibn Battuta never expected to see him again.

How lucky he was, he thought, to meet a person who could vouch for his credentials as the ambassador of Muhammad Shah! The passing of so much time did not seem to make any difference. He had accomplished the first part of his mission and reached China.

The emir greeted him warmly, introduced Ibn Battuta to the director of customs, and saw that he was given good lodgings in the section of the port area designated for merchants. The Muslim kadi, the sheikh, and a number of merchants called upon the Moor, among them a man from Tabriz who had been one of the traders lending Ibn Battuta goods at the time of his arrival in India. Now this man, delighted to see an old friend and noted traveler, was prepared to make him generous gifts. Indeed, Ibn Battuta found all the Muslim colony of Zaytun most willing to help him. These merchants were extremely wealthy and could well afford to be lavish in their hospitality.

Almost immediately Ibn Battuta learned that riches here were not counted in dinars and other gold coins, but in paper money. Chinese were the first nation to use banknotes, and the theory of paying for articles and services with flimsy bits of paper was hard for a stranger to comprehend. It was explained to the Moor that all the gold and silver coming into the country was cast in ingots. He discovered that buying and selling was carried on exclusively by means of pieces of paper, each the size of the palm of the hand and stamped with the sultan's seal. "Twenty-five of these take the place of a dinar with us," he related. "When these notes become torn by handling, one takes them to an office corresponding to our mint and receives their equivalent in new notes. If anyone goes to the bazaar with a silver dirhem or a dinar, intending to buy something, no one will accept it or pay any attention to him until he changes it for paper."

Ibn Battuta had become accustomed to the "slant" eyes, beardless faces, and general appearance of Chinese from having seen them in his travels, but he found many things about them astounding. For instance, although they manufactured extremely beautiful silk fabrics, this cloth, so costly elsewhere, had no special value and was worn by the poorest classes, whereas a rich merchant might be dressed in a coarse cotton tunic.

He found pork and dog flesh on sale in the markets, neither

of which meats a Muslim would eat. Marvelous to him was the sight of how the Chinese cooked and heated their houses with a burning stone. Coal was unknown in Arab lands, and Ibn Battuta could only describe it in relation to charcoal.

He was impressed with the skill of Chinese artists and discovered that, wherever he was to go in the country, he and his companions would be sketched unawares, and the portraits would be displayed in public places as part of a pictorial newsletter affixed to a wall. In the Arab lands, depicting the human figure was forbidden by the Koran, but here portraits were a part of public record. "If a stranger commits an offense," Ibn Battuta was told, "they send his picture far and wide, a search is made for him, and when the person resembling the portrait is found, he is arrested."

When the director of customs at Zaytun heard Ibn Battuta's story, he wrote to the Mongol emperor to inform him of the arrival of an ambassador from the sultan of India. While the Moor was waiting for the khan's reply to come from Peking, he asked leave to travel in the region around the city and for someone to accompany him on his trip through the southern portion of the realm. The request was granted, and by overland stages Ibn Battuta reached the country's inland water system, consisting of the tributaries and canals related to the Yangtze River system. He sailed mostly in a kind of galley with rowers standing in the center to ply their oars and the passengers accommodated in the forepart and stern. Awnings of a material like grass cloth (textile made chiefly from grass or other vegetable fiber) shaded the ship.

For twenty-seven days he journeyed on this river, the boat tying up each noon where supplies could be purchased at villages and mooring again at night. The Moor inspected the surrounding country as well as he could and was especially impressed when the vessel stopped at a city where porcelain was manufactured. He had seen dishes made of this substance in royal courts, but none he had been acquainted with were so fine.

He described the porcelain as being manufactured of the soil of certain mountains, which could be burned like charcoal. This earth, mixed with a stone and burned, so Ibn Battuta said, made a kind of clay that was allowed to ferment. This material became the exquisite dishes that were exported to distant lands.

His wanderings at this time are difficult to understand. In some manner he appears to have reached Canton. It was a leisurely journey and seems to have been a meandering one. He told of staying in a city where the Muslims showered gifts and entertainments on him, and he lived with a wealthy Muslim, remaining two weeks. He observed temples, markets, fruit orchards, hospitals, musicians—a never-ending kaleidoscope of sights to be recalled later to awed listeners.

After his return to Zaytun, the khan's order arrived. He was to be received at Peking and was to be conveyed there with full honors. Did he wish to go by land or water? He chose water transportation, so a splendid vessel was placed at his disposal, and he traveled as a state guest.

One of his first stops was Fuchow (present Linchwan), which had a pleasant setting on a garden-studded plain and reminded him of Damascus. He was met by the kadi, sheikh, and merchants, with musicians and a horse on which to ride into the city. Here he was treated as the sultan's guest and lodged at the house of the sheikh.

While he was still in Fuchow, a vessel came in bringing a reverend gentleman from Ceuta (a seaport in modern Morocco, near the Strait of Gibraltar and not far from Tangier), who asked to visit Ibn Battuta, as they were from the same country. Both wept at the sight of someone from the homeland. Then Ibn Battuta recalled that they had met before—in Delhi, where the man had been invited to remain at the court but had refused because he wished to go to China.

Ibn Battuta could not enthuse about this land. In spite of its agreeable features, China did not attract him. He felt very alien among the hordes of heathens. Sight of the monasteries and Buddhist priests, the huge families of the poor, their pigs, and the unorthodox manner in which they prepared their food distressed him so much that he often remained indoors rather than go out to inspect life in the streets.

"When I met Muslims in China, I always felt just as though I were meeting my own faith and kin," he said. Their kindness to him warmed his heart. He clung to the respected man from Ceuta who accompanied him for four days to another city where he owned several houses and had agents representing his business. Reluctantly the traveler bade his friend adieu, hating to leave this understanding man. A week in his company had been a nostalgic dip into the homeland so far away.

Now the vessel carried Ibn Battuta seventeen more days on to Hangchow, the largest city he had seen. It may well have been the largest in the world at that time. Until 1276 it had been the capital of the Sung dynasty. Many thousands of foreigners were settled there—Muslim, Jewish, and Christian. Hangchow was so great, Ibn Battuta said, it took three days to traverse it. It was divided in six walled sections, and each inhabitant had his own house and garden.

Again a party came out to meet the traveler, bringing drums, bugles, and trumpets. There were the kadi and sheikh and a principal Muslim family, also the governor and his escort. The Moor was lodged in a different house each of the first two nights. Then on the third day he was taken to the Muslim quarter, which was much like the surroundings in an Islamic country, with bazaars, a mosque, and muezzins calling to prayer. A wealthy Egyptian, who had built the mosque and endowed it, took the Moor into his mansion, and after that Ibn Battuta was a guest every night at some entertainment. During the fifteen days he remained he was treated to many pleasure rides in the daytime. There were numerous Muslims in Hangchow, and Ibn Battuta no longer experienced that yearning for home he had so recently felt.

On one of his rides he was taken to call on the governor. In the crowded street he became separated from his companions when the vizier passed by with a large suite. Knowing who Ibn Battuta was, the vizier asked if everything had been to the traveler's satisfaction. He would not hear of the Moor joining his companions before being taken to the governor. Ibn Battuta that day was wearing the mohair mantle Sheikh Jalal ad-Din of Tabriz had given him in Assam, and the ruler was attracted to it.

"Take your mantle off," he ordered.

Ibn Battuta protested, but the governor insisted on giving him ten robes in place of the cloak, also a horse, harness, and money.

The Moor seethed with anger because of the loss of the cloak, which had been the present of a holy man, but when he had time to reflect, he recalled the prediction that an infidel sultan would seize it.

After all, the ruler greatly extended himself to show Ibn Battuta hospitality, playing host to him in the palace three days, arranging a banquet at which all the food was prepared according to Muslim ritual, and entertaining him with a mock battle and musical performance on the water.

That same night when he was taken back to the palace, there was a performance. The audience was seated in the middle of the palace courtyard, for it was the season of extreme heat. The ruler called in a slave juggler and commanded, "Show us some of your feats."

The man took a wooden ball in which there were holes and long leather thongs and threw it in the air. It rose out of sight of the audience, but a piece of cord remained in the man's hand, and he ordered an apprentice to climb up the rope. The youth did so and disappeared. The juggler called three times and, receiving no reply, took a knife as if he were enraged and climbed up the rope until he too disappeared. Then in a few seconds a boy's hand was tossed down, after that a foot, another hand, next the youth's body, and finally his head.

Out of the void descended the man, puffing and blowing,

his clothes smeared with blood. He was a grisly sight. The performer kissed the ground in front of the ruler, who issued an order. Whereupon the juggler gathered up the boy's limbs, placed them so they touched each other, gave the body a kick, and the youth rose up, sound as ever.

Ibn Battuta watched this performance, his heart palpitating. He had no liking for gruesome acts, but he had witnessed a similar performance in India. This was much more realistic, and he was so upset that the courtiers brought him a drink of some liquid. The kadi, sitting beside him, grasped Ibn Battuta by the hand reassuringly and exclaimed, "By God, there was no climbing or coming down or cutting up of limbs at all. The whole thing is just hocus-pocus."

The Moor never forgot the chilling sight of the boy's body coming down piecemeal from above. He carried back to the Western world the first report of what is still known to magicians as the oriental rope trick.

On the day after this entertainment Ibn Battuta was guest of the governor of the fifth and largest quarter of Hangchow, and on the following day he visited the sixth, or port sector of the city, inhabited by seamen, fishermen, caulkers, carpenters, and soldiers. Here a vessel was fitted up for the next part of his journey, and he departed for the land of Cathay, as northern China was called then.

He was sixty-four days on the way to Peking by the unknown route he followed. He said nothing about whether he sailed by the Yellow Sea and the Gulf of Chihli or the mouth of the Hai River and the Grand Canal, or whether he followed an inland river. There was much he did not understand about the geography of China, the language was incomprehensible to him, place names were confusing, and he prepared his memoirs a whole decade after he had left there. So he had little to say about the country except for its Muslim communities.

What he saw of Cathay was a heavily cultivated region.

Fruit orchards and gardens, green fields, and villages extended the entire distance inland to Peking (then called Khan-Baliq, "the city of the Mongol khan"). Western writers of that era called it Cambaluc.

The boat moored ten miles outside the city, and a written report was sent to the authorities, who gave the visitors permission to disembark and enter. Ibn Battuta observed at this place that the gardens were entirely outside the high walls, and the khan's city lay in their center like a citadel.

As Muslims were few in this place, Ibn Battuta immediately sought out the convent of Sheikh Burhan ad-Din, about whom he had long been told. The khan had made Burhan head of the scanty group of followers of Islam who lived in his territories.

When shown into the room where the sheikh was reading, Ibn Battuta was astonished to see that his host was wearing the identical mohair mantle that the sultan in Hangchow had demanded of him.

When the greetings were over, Ibn Battuta fingered the cloak, still questioning if it could possibly be the one he had worn.

"Why examine it when you know it already?" the sheikh said, his eyes reflecting his amusement.

Ibn Battuta explained about receiving such a robe from Jalal ad-Din, whereupon Sheikh Burhan said he knew all about the circumstances, that Jalal had made the robe expressly for him and foretold how it would reach him at Peking.

"Jalal ad-Din," he added, "could do much more than this in the way of making predictions, but now I have been told he has passed to the mercy of God."

The holy man had disappeared, it was said, and no one knew what had become of him.

Ibn Battuta was not destined to be presented to the Mongol khan. The monarch was absent from the city, putting down a rebellion in country three months' journey distant.

Meanwhile after his departure the majority of his emirs had thrown off their allegiance and agreed to depose the khan. There had been a battle, and news was received a few days after the Moor's arrival that the ruler had been defeated and killed.

This was the signal for rejoicing, the capital was decorated, trumpets, bugles, and drums were played in the streets, and games and entertainments were held for a month. The slain khan's body arrived, with the bodies of about a hundred of his relatives and courtiers who had also been killed. A great tomb was prepared for him and richly furnished. Now that he was dead in battle, his enemies could afford to give him a funeral of honor. Gold and silver plate were brought from the palace for burial with him. Also four slave girls and six principal warriors were to be buried alive in the tomb. The burial chamber was walled up, and earth was piled around it until it became a great mound. Four horses were run around the grave until exhausted, then they were impaled on wooden stakes. Bodies of the dead courtiers were also placed in subterranean chambers along with their weapons and house utensils, and horses were impaled over their tombs.

It was a barbaric spectacle, which the entire populace was expected to attend. Even the Muslims were required to be there, wearing long white garments.

The khan's ladies and courtiers set up camp near the grave and lived on the site forty days or more, a bazaar being established to provide their food.

After the ceremonial funeral disorders broke out in Cathay of such serious proportions that Sheikh Burhan ad-Din summoned Ibn Battuta and expressed fears for his safety.

"You had better return to southern China before the disturbances become worse," he advised. "Go quickly."

This was likewise the opinion of the khan's successor, for he sent three men to escort the Moor back down the river and ensure his treatment as a royal guest. As he fled from this baffling country, Ibn Battuta must have been anxious about the chances of his crossing the world again and safely reaching his native land. He had been through so many adventures to get to Cathay, would he have to survive more frightful experiences on the way home?

He had not exactly performed Muhammad Shah's commission, but he had spent a year in China trying to do so. He went back to Fuchow and Zaytun (this route indicates that he made the trip by inland waterways), and when he reached the coast, he found a number of junks about to sail for India. To his great relief, among them was a vessel with a Muslim crew, which he learned belonged to the sultan of Sumatra, where he had had such good relations with the ruler. The sultan's agent was acquainted with Ibn Battuta and invited him to be a passenger on the craft. Nothing could have suited the traveler better. He had by then endured his fill of infidel surroundings.

Thus he said good-bye to the mysterious land of the Mongol khans. He had witnessed many rare sights and had ventured beyond the fringe of Muslim influence. Tucked in his memory were wonders to describe on that faraway day when —or if—he should again be back in his own country.

It was now the last half of the year 1346. He had been gone from home twenty-one years, half his life span. His thoughts were strongly turned toward the Maghreb, but the question was: Would he ever reach his native land? Thus far predictions of holy men had seemed to govern his fate, but there had been no prophecies to assure him of a safe return.

XIII
Homeward Again by Junk— The Black Death

At first the junk sailed for ten days with fair winds, then the sky darkened, rain fell, the breeze shifted, and the vessel was blown off its course. The crew became alarmed because the sun did not poke through the clouds, and they did not know where they were. Sailors clamored to return to the China coast, but the captain disregarded all pleas and continued into unknown waters.

On the forty-third day at sea a mountain was spied rising out of the water some distance away. It looked like nothing known to the mariners, and fear increased. The ship seemed to be heading directly toward it, carried by the wind, and it appeared as though the junk would be cast upon this alien shore and wrecked. Being good Muslims, everyone prayed, and the wealthy merchants aboard vowed to distribute large sums in alms if they were saved. They requested Ibn Battuta to write down their pledges, which he did, being one of the few persons there who possessed skill with calligraphy.

Thus passed an anxious day with the threatening peak looming ahead and all of the passengers placing their lives in the hands of God.

Next morning dawned, the wind died down, the sky cleared, and there was no mountain anywhere on the horizon. It had been a mirage. Nevertheless, there were many men on board who were sure they had seen a manifestation of the roc—a supernatural bird that belonged to Arab legend.

Two months later the junk reached Sumatra and landed at the port where Ibn Battuta had previously been. Of course the sultan remembered him. The ruler had just returned from a raid that had netted a large number of captives, so he presented the Moor with two slave girls and two boys. (The island of Sumatra was divided into eight kingdoms then; it had a wild interior and was not a completely peaceful place.)

During the two months Ibn Battuta waited on Sumatra for another vessel, the sultan lodged him in style. Then he sent him aboard a junk that was carrying a gift of aloeswood, camphor, cloves, and sandalwood to Quilon. On this aromatic vessel he made his way to familiar territory at the southwestern tip of India, the passage occupying forty days. Travel was extremely slow by sail, even with the winds blowing in a favorable direction.

Ibn Battuta considered returning to Delhi and reporting to Muhammad Shah the details of his embassy to the absent Mongol khan, but the more he thought of it, the more he feared the powerful, bloodthirsty sultan. How would Muhammad Shah receive him? While the monsoons blew toward the Yemen coast, he decided he had better get out of India, so at the end of April, 1347, he embarked instead in a craft bound for Dhofar (in Hadhramaut, southern coast of Arabia).

He continued from there around the coast of Oman, up the south side of the Gulf of Hormuz, thence to Hormuz itself and on to Shiraz in Iran. He was going over old territory—Isfahan, Basra, and Baghdad, arriving at the last city in January. Of the ten months it took him to cover that distance from India he left no details of his travels, but it is thought that some of his memories of earlier wanderings over the same routes may have rightly belonged to his second journey through Iran and Iraq.

At Baghdad he encontered a man from Morocco who told him bad news about the defeat of the Moorish sultan's army at Tarifa (on the Spanish side of Gibraltar) and the capture of Algeciras, Spain, by the Christians. This had happened a good many years earlier, in 1340 and 1342, but it was fresh information to Ibn Battuta. He had been away a long time.

Ibn Battuta went up the Euphrates Valley into Syria, heading for Damascus, which he had last seen twenty years ago. How good it seemed to him to be approaching through the miles of gardens encircling the place. He had special interest in revisiting the city, for lately he had realized that he was a man much alone in the world. For all his marriages and the slave women he had had in his harem, he mentioned only two children of his own—the infant girl who died in India and the little boy who remained with his mother in the Maldive Islands. Now he was going to learn if he had a son in Damascus.

When he had last been there, he left behind a pregnant wife who no longer wished to accompany him and endure the hardships of travel on horse- and camelback. While in India he was told she had given birth to a boy who would be a young man by now. Ibn Battuta looked forward to finding him and tasting the joys of fatherhood. Would this youth have any of the Moor's interests? Would he be a scholar?

Ibn Battuta began his search at the principal mosque and by good fortune came upon an imam he had known a score of years ago. The man did not recognize the pilgrim at first, but when the traveler spoke of the twenty-two days he had spent sitting at lectures and how the professor had taken the needy young man home when he was ill, the imam remembered He knew also that the wife had died soon afterward.

"And the son," he said, "your boy has been dead these twelve years."

This was not the only blow to Ibn Battuta's hopes. The imam sent him to a scholar from Tangier who was living in Damascus.

"Perhaps he can tell you of your family."

That he could, for the Battutas had been well known. The scholar said, "Your father died fifteen years ago, but your mother was still alive when I left the city."

Ibn Battuta could shut his eyes and see his parents the day he left Tangier on his horse, when they stood outside the gate of the low stucco house watching as he rode down the narrow street. That had been his last glimpse of them. He had so often thought of returning and seeing their eyes glow with pride as he told of his wanderings and the courts where he had been honorably received. Had anyone carried news of him to his parents? There had been no way to communicate with them except by word of mouth. With a wrench he reflected on how it must have seemed to them for a son to disappear into the great void, the unknown world of the East.

A somewhat saddened man, he stayed on in Damascus until the end of the year 1348. In that city he was regarded as a revered scholar, traveler, and pilgrim, but there was no great bounty for him in remaining, as times were hard and a scarcity of provisions existed. He left for the seacoast by way of Homs and Aleppo (in present Syria), the route he had found so interesting on his former visits. Arriving at the latter city, he learned of a great epidemic that had broken out in the western part of the world. The bubonic plague, or Black Death, was ahead of him. It was said that at Gaza over a thousand persons had died in one day. Alarmed, Ibn Battuta turned back toward Damascus, where it was still safe, but when he reached Homs, the epidemic had raced ahead of him, and three hundred persons succumbed in that city the day of his arrival.

At Damascus fear reigned, and the inhabitants were fasting three days. Then they went in a procession, carrying the Koran and going to pray at the Mosque of the Footprints of Moses south of the city. The Jews with their Book of the Law and Christians with their Gospels joined the supplicants. Ibn Battuta followed the great concourse and took part in the services in which all ranks of the population pleaded for God's help in the impending calamity.

"It seemed that God heard their pleas," the Moor related afterward, "and lightened their affliction."

Not as many died in Damascus as in the Egyptian cities. But Ibn Battuta could not escape the epidemic—it seemed to prevail everywhere. He went to Jerusalem, where the disease had already passed through, and there were no longer deaths from it. His homeward path took him to Gaza, the greater part of which seemed depopulated. He hurried on through Damietta to Alexandria (both in present Egypt), where the peak of the epidemic had passed. At Cairo he learned that 21,000 died in a single day. The figures he gathered about the disastrous toll of the plague are believed not to have been exaggerated. He was spared from catching the disease and survived a terrible period. This may be why he decided to make one more pilgrimage to Mecca, to express to God in fitting terms his thankfulness for having escaped.

He made the round trip and came back to Egypt, where he again received word of his native land. It was heartening because he heard that its ruler had united his scattered forces after numerous petty revolts and intrigues, and the reign of Sultan Abu'l-Hasan had been one of prosperity and benevolence. Ibn Battuta was led to feel that he could lead a good life in Morocco, where he understood scholarship was encouraged. Moved by memories of his boyhood, a deep love of his native land, and a yearning to see his mother and old friends, he lost no time in seeking a means of completing his return journey.

Before leaving Alexandria he again visited the Pharos and was sorry it appeared more ruinous than before. He could not enter the lower part of the tower or even climb up over the rubble to the door.

Ibn Battuta engaged passage in a small trading vessel that was leaving the Egyptian coast in May, 1349, and traveled in it as far as Djerba off southeastern Tunisia. It was lucky he went ashore when he did, for the ship was captured by enemy Christian pirates before it reached Tunis.

He next found a small boat to take him to Gabes and from there to Sfax (both in present Tunisia). Then he went by land with some Arabs to Tunis, where he remained thirty-six days before boarding a Spanish vessel that carried him to the port of Cagliari in Sardinia. Its citizens were noted for their piratical inclinations, and the Moor had a feeling that although he was getting near home, he wasn't going to make it to his destination.

"I made a vow to God to fast for two successive months if He should deliver us from this island," he said. "Because we found out that its inhabitants were intending to pursue us when we left and take us captive."

Truly the final lap of his great journey seemed more fraught with perils than any dangers he had encountered in the East. The vessel got away all right, but when Ibn Battuta left the boat at Tlemcen (in present Algeria near its border with Morocco), he ran into more hazards. He was traveling by road on this part of the trip and had spent the first night out in a hermitage. He was at this time accompanied by another pilgrim and his brother. He was nearly within the bounds of his own country, and if he had a false sense of security, it was because he had forgotten the bands of tribal raiders who roamed the frontier. Suddenly after leaving the hermitage, the little party was attacked by fifty men on foot and two horsemen.

"We resolved to make a fight for it and put up a flag," he later related.

The raiders, seeing that there were two pilgrims in the group, relented, made peace with the travelers, and offered to escort them part of the way. So they reached Taza, safe inside Morocco, and found acquaintances. Here Ibn Battuta was told of his mother's death from the plague. He sensed a great loss. There was no relative for him to go back to after all. His homecoming was not what he had visualized, and this was only one of the many discouraging circumstances that dogged his return.

He arrived at the royal city of Fez on November 13, 1349, almost exactly twenty-four years and eight months since he had departed from Tangier. Confidently, he presented himself before Sultan Abu Inan, who had recently overthrown his father. Ibn Battuta endeavored to make a good impression on the monarch by extolling his works and saying they excelled those of the many other sultans he had met.

As a pilgrim, with five visits to the holy shrine of Mecca to his credit, Ibn Battuta was entitled to respect, but when he spoke of the eastern lands, much of what he had to say was received with skepticism. Arabs had a taste for colorful and marvelous tales, but listeners thought the traveler took his narratives too seriously. Envious courtiers declared he was a boaster and big talker. Some branded him a plain liar.

This was not what Ibn Battuta had anticipated of his fellow countrymen. His pride was hurt, and so he left the capital and went to visit his mother's tomb in Tangier, then he looked up friends in Ceuta, where he fell ill.

It was three months before he recovered and restlessly pondered what to do with himself. In the past he had always had a goal. Now he was just another returned pilgrim whom people considered afflicted with a wild imagination. He no longer had an entourage—companions and slaves. He was a lone man again, one whom some persons regarded as having strange fantasies, perhaps a little touched in the head.

Who could stomach the tales of marvels he related? Who could believe that Sultan Muhammad Shah once stationed elephants with catapults on their backs to fling gold and silver coins to the populace while he marched from the city gates to the palace?

Men called the Moor a rogue and a prevaricator, an imposter weaving tales for the sake of causing a sensation.

One day he was relating a fanciful story about black stones which he asserted the inhabitants of China burned to heat their houses. When someone questioned the veracity of this statement, he had the effrontery to reply, "I have warmed myself with these burning stones. The Chinese bring the lumpy earth from the mountains, break it up, and set it on fire. It gives more heat than charcoal."

When men would have cast the rogue out, the caliph apparently tolerated him for the sake of entertainment. Those who had received him at first with honor accused him of avarice or called him crazy. One person, they pointed out, could not have been in so many places, nor was it likely he would have been received by so many rulers.

Well, there still remained one member of Ibn Battuta's family who might believe him. He had a cousin in Spain, a learned kadi, who surely would relish the traveler's accounts of wise and holy men he had visisted in the far corners of the world.

Spain was close by, and it was one section of the Islamic lands Ibn Battuta had not seen. Morocco was still conducting holy wars there, and King Alfonso XI had besieged Gibraltar for ten months in his effort to drive the Moors out of Andalusia. Alfonso was now dead of the plague, and Sultan Abu Inan's father had strengthened the fortifications of the famous

Rock, and Abu Inan had gone on improving them, so that when Ibn Battuta saw the place its defenses were a marvel of ingenuity.

Ibn Battuta went inland to Ronda, situated on a high cliff in the mountains, and spent five days with his cousin, then set out to see a little more of Andalusia. He followed a rough road back to the coast at Marbela, where he found a company of horsemen bound for the seaport of Málaga. He arranged to accompany them, but they left ahead of him. Afterward he thought what had seemed his misfortune was the hand of God interfering in his behalf, for when he galloped out to catch up with them, he observed a couple of suspicious circumstances. He passed a dead horse lying in a ditch and a little farther on a pannier of fish thrown on the ground. These seemed to indicate a need for caution, so he left the road and went to a house, where he found another dead horse.

While he was still at the house, he heard shouting and turned back to where some soldiers were gathered. The commander told him four galleys of Christians had appeared and landed men on the coast, who had attacked the horsemen with whom Ibn Battuta had intended traveling. One man had been killed, ten taken prisoners, and one had escaped. A fisherman had been killed in the fight, and that was his basket.

The officer took Ibn Battuta under his protection as far as Málaga, where the kadi and other principal citizens were gathered in the great mosque collecting money to ransom the prisoners. Ibn Battuta thanked God that he was not one of the missing men.

From this city he went on to Granada, where he intended to present himself to the Moorish sultan, but the latter was ill, so Ibn Battuta never saw the famous Alhambra palace. The ruler's mother, with true Muslim beneficence, sent him some gold dinars. "Of which I made good use," he said. He surely needed them by this time. Here he was received with the kind of honor to which he had become accustomed on his travels. He met several distinguished scholars and spent some days with the principal sheikh in his hermitage.

Andalusia seemed very beautiful to the Moor. He specially admired the fertility of its gardens. When he left, his route was back through Málaga, Ronda, and Gibraltar. He crossed the strait to Ceuta and wandered aimlessly through several other Moroccan cities. There was growing on him a realization that one more section of the Muslim world remained which he had not yet seen. Since he had set himself a goal to travel through all of it, the high road beckoned him again.

There was no reason for him to remain in his homeland, where he seemed to merit little honor, so for his own satisfaction he would travel once more. He would not leave Africa, and he would not go as far away as Egypt, yet he would visit places almost completely unknown. The Muslim Mandingo tribe, he learned, had recently built a powerful Negro empire on a great inland river (the Niger), and this would be his objective.

With his usual cleverness he managed to recoup his finances and equip himself for the journey. The plan met with the sultan's approval, and Ibn Battuta traveled from Marrakech to Fez (both in present Morocco) in the ruler's suite before he set out for the Negro lands. He was confident that, if anything would restore him to general esteem, it was this journey —one close to home and yet feared because of the terrible desert crossing that lay ahead of him.

Ibn Battuta was not afraid. At forty-eight he was still at heart an adventurer. He would show the scoffers his mettle!

XIV
Across the Sahara in Quest
of the Negro Lands

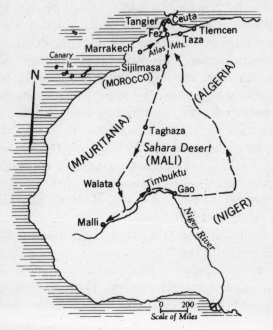

Whole books have been written about the trials of crossing the Sahara Desert, and to this very day men are essaying new ventures in that great waste of sand. The Sahara from time immemorial separated the Mediterranean civilization from the black countries where man lived thousands of years ago.

The Sahara's extent is almost as great as that of Europe minus the Scandinavian countries, and its breadth ranges up to 1,400 miles. Its winds are very dry, there is almost no rain, and oases are far apart. Its inhabitants in the Middle Ages were nomads, and they were in control of the only desert commerce, which was in salt and ivory.

There were no scientific exploring expeditions in Ibn Battuta's day, no learned anthropologists with the curiosity to penetrate the mysterious hinterland of continental Africa. So here he was unique, a persistent seeker of knowledge—though he was no professional geographer or mapmaker, merely a man with a great bump of inquisitiveness.

When he took leave of Sultan Abu Inan's suite at Fez, he rode horseback to Sijilmasa in southern Morocco, the principal trading post south of the Atlas Mountains (near modern Tafilelt), and remained with the brother of the learned Muslim from Ceuta he had met in Fuchow, China. While in the Moroccan town the traveler made his arrangements, purchasing camels and a four months' food supply.

On February 18, 1352, he set out with a caravan partly made up of merchants of Sijilmasa. They rode slightly southwest through the sand dunes for twenty-five days. Their objective was a strange little community called Taghaza (Terhazza in present Mali), where the buildings were made of blocks of salt roofed with camel skins. No trees were around the place, only miles and miles of sand. Beneath this sand the inhabitants dug for salt, finding it in thick slabs that looked as though they had been squared with tools and laid under the surface.

Only slaves lived at Taghaza, working the salt deposits and existing on a diet of dates, camel flesh, and millet, brought from the Negro lands to the south. The salt, Ibn Battuta learned, was carried away to the kingdom of Malli (located in the south of present Mali) and other places, the slabs being loaded two to a camel's back.

The party he was with remained at the village ten uncomfortable days, enduring brackish water and a plague of flies. They laid in a supply of water for an additional ten days' crossing of the sands, though later they found a pool of sweet rainwater, where they quenched their thirst more satisfactorily and were able to wash clothing.

Ibn Battuta learned odd facts about desert travel, that in places the sands swarmed with lice and that truffles grew plentifully and could be an addition to the food supply.

It was the custom for a member of the caravan to travel

ahead of the others and locate suitable pasturage for the beasts. When one of these scouts got lost and never returned, Ibn Battuta refrained from volunteering for this duty. From a passing caravan he heard of other men similarly lost, and one day his party found a fellow dead in the shade of a small shrub. He was only a mile from water.

At another well the caravan stopped three days to rest, the camelmen mending and filling waterskins and sewing over them covers of sackcloth to keep the wind from drying them out. A messenger was sent with letters to notify various persons in Walata (Oualata in present Mauritania) to expect the caravan and provide lodging for its members. Those who had no friend to write to communicated with a reputable merchant. It was expected that the recipients of the letters would send a party four nights' journey into the desert to meet the caravan and supply it with water.

Sometimes, said Ibn Battuta, the messenger perished before reaching his destination, and no one was apprised of the caravan's approach, which meant that the travelers were in danger of dying before they reached Walata.

"That desert is really haunted by demons," the Moor declared. "If the messenger is alone, they make sport of him and disorder his mind, so that he loses his way and perishes. There is no visible road or track in these parts, nothing but sand blown hither and thither by the wind. You see hills of it in one place, and afterwards you will see them moved to quite another place. Any guide to the sands has to be a man gifted with quick intelligence. I found it strange that the guide we had was blind in one eye and diseased in the other, yet he had the best knowledge of the road of any man."

It was a joyful occasion when, seven days out of the last stopping place, they saw the fires of the men who had come to meet the caravan. The party arrived at Walata two months after having set out. In this northernmost province of the Negroes, Ibn Battuta met a very different sort from the men who had been so hospitable in Mogadiscio and Kilwa.

On arrival in the town the merchants unloaded their goods in an open square, and blacks were posted to guard the merchandise while the travelers reported to the sultan's deputy. They found him sitting on a carpet under an archway, surrounded by guards carrying lances and bows. The official spoke to the merchants through an interpreter. There was every indication of his contempt for the white strangers, and Ibn Battuta already repented having gone to Walata because of the ill manners of the authorities.

In the city was a citizen of Rabat to whom Ibn Battuta had written requesting that he hire lodgings for him. A few days after he was settled in the house, a black official invited the members of the caravan to partake of his hospitality. Ibn Battuta would have declined, but his companions urged him to accompany them. A meal was served to the visitors consisting of pounded millet, honey, and milk, placed in a bowl-shaped gourd. The guests were expected to drink this mixture and retire.

Ibn Battuta was completely disgusted. "Was it for this that the black invited us?" he asked fellow travelers.

"Yes," a merchant told him. "They consider it the highest form of hospitality."

Ibn Battuta was so displeased he would have returned to Morocco at once with a pilgrim caravan that was about to leave Walata. However, he reconsidered and decided that since he had come this far and endured so much hardship to get there, he would go on to the capital of the king at Malli (present Nyani).

In the fifty days he remained at Walata the heat was excessive. The town boasted a few date palms, in the shade of which watermelons were grown. Sheep were raised, and mutton was available for food.

Although the inhabitants were Muslims, they were a strange breed. They claimed descent from their mother, not their father. The women went unveiled, and their families did not permit them to travel with their husbands though they were allowed other men friends besides their spouses. When Ibn Battuta called on the kadi, he was shocked to find a remarkably beautiful young woman with him.

Ibn Battuta turned to leave, and the kadi asked, "Why are you going out? She is my companion."

The Moor could not understand this conduct in a theologian and pilgrim. He should have known better, Ibn Battuta thought. Arab women were not exhibited publicly.

It was with relief that he made ready to leave for Malli, twenty-four days distant from Walata. He hired a guide and set out with three companions on a road that passed huge baobab trees. A traveler did not carry money or provisions in this country, but supplied himself with pieces of salt and glass ornaments to be traded with blacks, who brought out fruits, millet, milk, chickens, pounded beans, and the ingredients of couscous.

Eventually the party arrived at a large river, which Ibn Battuta mistakenly believed to be the upper Nile. He was not aware of the existence of the Niger, which it was. From its banks he saw his first crocodile. One day he was about to make a comfort stop when a black stepped between him and the river. Ibn Battuta was offended that this man should intrude upon a very private matter, but when he spoke to his companions of the fellow's lack of manners, someone informed him, "You should be grateful. His purpose was solely to protect you from the crocodile."

Ibn Battuta realized he would have to be more discriminating about choosing spots in which to relieve himself, otherwise he would become a meal for the river monsters.

As in approaching Walata, it was the custom at Malli to write ahead and secure permission to enter, also to arrange for hire of a house. Accordingly, Ibn Battuta inquired for a certain Arab trader, and the man's son-in-law appeared at once, bringing gifts of candles and food. Next day the trader and other prominent residents called, among them a black kadi who was a pilgrim of excellent character. The Muslims of Malli, aware of Islamic customs of hospitality, generously supplied presents for Ibn Battuta. All was going well for him until ten days later he and his companions ate some of the country's most popular dish, a gruel made from a root resembling dasheen, or taro. The entire group became violently ill, one of them dying. After the Moor fainted at morning prayer, he asked an Egyptian, who had some medical knowledge, if he could provide a remedy. The man gave him a mixture of a vegetable root, aniseed, sugar, and water. Ibn Battuta drank the potion, vomited repeatedly, and felt better, but it was two months before he was over the illness.

While sick he could not pay his customary call upon the sultan, but he was told the ruler was miserly, and there was no chance of receiving a rich present from him. Later the sultan of Malli gave a banquet to which doctors, the kadi, preacher, and other dignitaries were invited. Ibn Battuta went along with the theologians and listened while the Koran was read and prayers were said in behalf of the ruler. After the ceremony he saluted the sultan, the kadi, and preacher, explaining that he was a noted traveler and pilgrim.

By means of an interpreter the ruler told him to give thanks. Ibn Battuta did not know just why, but he dutifully recited, "Praise be to God and thanks under all circumstances."

Shortly he learned that the sultan was sending him a present at the kadi's house. From past experience he expected it to consist of robes of honor and money.

He stood up to receive the gift and was amazed when messengers from the court thrust into his hands three loaves of bread, a piece of beef fried in oil, and a calabash full of sour curds. So this was a royal hospitality gift!

The Moor could not suppress his laughter. "I thought it a most amazing thing," he commented, "that they could be so foolish and make so much of such a paltry matter."

Two months went by with no further beneficences from

his royal highness, although the Moor went frequently to the palace and sat by the kadi and preacher at audiences. The court interpreter had been exceedingly friendly with Ibn Battuta, and in the season of Ramadan he counseled, "If you are dissatisfied with the sultan's ideas of Muslim hospitality, speak out in his presence, and I shall express to him on your behalf whatever is necessary."

The holy time of the year appeared to offer a propitious moment, and Ibn Battuta rose during the audience and addressed the sultan.

"I have traveled through the countries of the world," he said, "and have met their rulers. I have been four months in your country, yet you have neither shown me real hospitality nor given me anything. What am I to say of you before other rulers?"

"I have not seen you before and have not been told about you," the sultan responded.

Two of Ibn Battuta's friends rose and informed the ruler, "He has already saluted you, and you have sent him food."

Apparently this statement impressed the sultan with his Muslim obligations. He ordered a house set apart for the guest and a daily sum to be paid for his expenses. On the Night of Power, when he distributed alms to the kadi and theologians, he included thirteen gold miskals for Ibn Battuta.

On certain days the sultan held audiences in the palace yard amid great pomp. Clad in a velvety red tunic, carrying a bow in one hand and a quiver on his back, and wearing on his head a golden skullcap bound with a golden band with long knife-shaped ends, the ruler mounted three steps to a platform on which cushions were placed. It was shaded by a great silken umbrella surmounted with a large golden bird. Musicians preceded him, playing two-stringed guitars, and behind marched three hundred armed slaves. Two saddled and bridled horses were brought in, likewise two goats as protection against the evil eye.

Ibn Battuta observed that anyone summoned to appear before the sultan had to remove his customary clothing, don worn garments and a dirty skullcap, then go forward in an attitude of humility, knocking the ground with his elbows, then standing with bowed head and bent back. If the sultan gave the man a favorable reply or spoke graciously, the supplicant uncovered his back and threw dust over it and over his head. The Moor wondered that these men did not blind themselves doing so, but this was their idea of good court manners.

He told of other odd court ceremonies, particularly how on a Muslim feast day poets appeared before the sultan's platform, wearing costumes and wooden headpieces in complete imitation of thrushes with red beaks and an outer coating of feathers.

"In this ridiculous makeup, like great birds they stand in front of the sultan and recite their poems," he said. "The verses are like sermons listing good deeds of the sultan and those who preceded him. I am told this is a very old custom amongst them and was followed before their introduction to Islam, nevertheless they have kept it up."

Although the sultan had a reputation for stinginess, on the day of the Moor's departure, he surprised his guest with another gift of a hundred miskals.

Ibn Battuta had some good things to say of the country. It gave one a feeling of complete security. Misdeeds were so severely punished that there was nothing to fear from robbers or violent wrongdoers. If a white man died, his property was not confiscated but was cared for by responsible persons until the rightful heir was found. The Negroes were assiduous in observing the hours of prayer and training their children to learn the Koran by heart. They all wore clean white garments to the mosque on Fridays.

But there were bad things too. The nakedness of the women was especially offensive to Ibn Battuta, as was the eating of dog and ass meat. He did not like the custom of throwing dust or ashes over men's heads as a mark of respect nor did he care for their other grotesque ceremonies.

Altogether Ibn Battuta spent eight months in Malli, leaving on February 27, 1353, with a merchant, both riding camels. That night they arrived at a wide branch of the Niger River —he still thought it was the Nile—where it was necessary to cross in boats. On reaching this spot Ibn Battuta saw sixteen enormous beasts in the water and supposed they were elephants. "No," the merchant told him, "they are hippopotami which have come out of the river to go to pastures on shore."

The animals lifted their heads and blew, and the boatmen were afraid the hippos would sink their craft, therefore they kept close to shore. If they hunted the great creatures, they used spears with a hole bored in them through which heavy cords were passed. The spear was aimed at the animal's neck or head. If it found its mark and went through, then the men pulled on the rope, bringing the beast to the bank and butchering it. Ibn Battuta said the shore of the river was strewn with the bones.

Shortly after this Ibn Battuta's camel died, and to his disgust, it was immediately eaten by the blacks. He had to wait six days until another mount could be obtained, then he and the merchant went on to Timbuktu (in present Mali), where most of the inhabitants belonged to a tribe wearing face veils.

He reported little about this fabled city, although he remained several days. From there he boarded a small boat hollowed from a single piece of wood. It stopped each night so that the travelers could go ashore in villages and purchase their needs, using salt, spices, and glass beads for money. At one place a huge black man was governor.

"I needed some millet," Ibn Battuta related, "so I visited him while in the town—it was the Prophet's birthday. He took me by the hand and led me into his audience hall, where I was given a drink made of water containing pounded millet mixed with a little honey or milk. Afterward a green melon was brought in. A young boy entered, and the governor said, 'Here is your hospitality gift. Keep an eye on him in case he escapes.' "

The boy did not run away. He accompanied Ibn Battuta on the rest of his journey and remained with him for years.

Ibn Battuta continued down the Niger River to Gao (in present Mali), which he regarded as one of the best towns of the Negro lands. It had a variety of foodstuffs, and trading there was done with cowrie shells. He stayed about a month and then turned away from the river and set out eastward with a large merchant caravan, whose leader was a black pilgrim. They were now in the country of the Tuaregs, a tribe of Berbers, where a guarantee of protection was needed and where the women, though beautiful, were very stout. Ibn Battuta was sick from stomach trouble and the heat—this region was only 16 degrees north of the equator.

At the next big town (in the central region of Niger) he wished to meet the sultan, who was living a day's journey out from the city. The Moor hired a guide and went to call on the ruler. The latter was told about the traveler and came to meet him, riding a horse with a gorgeous saddlecloth and wearing a blue cloak, trousers, and turban.

He asked the Moor's story and on hearing it, lodged him in a tent, sent him a roasted sheep and a wooden bowl of cow's milk. These people ate no cereal foods nor even knew about them. Ibn Battuta remained at the encampment six days and on departing received a camel and ten gold miskals as gifts.

When he returned to the town, he was greeted with a disturbing message from the sultan of Morocco, commanding him to go back to his capital. Such a thing had never happened before, and the traveler did not know what it portended, whether good or bad developments for him. He purchased two riding camels and provisions for seventy days and prepared for the journey, departing on September 11 with a large caravan that included six hundred women slaves. (The region where he had been was a trading area, one of its principal commodities being slaves.)

At first the long procession traveled through pasture lands, then they arrived at the edge of the uninhabited, waterless desert. After a time the route divided, the east branch taking off for Egypt. The caravan crossed into southern Algeria, where there were more men wearing face veils. A Berber chief held up the caravan until he was paid pieces of cloth and other goods. It was again the month of Ramadan, and robbers and raiders ceased to molest travelers during the holy period.

They passed through stony and inhospitable places and into a marsh country where dates grew and locusts were one of the principal foods—the inhabitants went out before sunrise to catch them. Ibn Battuta stopped at Buda to wait to join another caravan bound for Sijilmasa (in today's Tafilalet oasis in Algeria). His road led him through the rugged Atlas Mountains. It was the end of December and so cold that heavy snow fell, making the road worse than any he had traveled in Bukhara or Khorasan. However, he was almost at his destination, though still anxious as to why the sultan had summoned him. He entered Fez in trepidation, only to find an unexpectedly pleasant welcome. Instead of facing a dire situation, he discovered that this last journey had been close enough to home so that he was believed by even the most skeptical, and he was told at once that the sultan had an agreeable task on the agenda for him.

This was the kind of return he had always hoped for. Sultan Abu Inan announced he had made arrangements to provide the traveler with a scribe and preserve his story. What Ibn Battuta had to tell of the hazardous crossings of the Sahara and the lands on its other side might be of great use. His determination to complete his travels through all the Islamic countries had been convincingly demonstrated, and members of the court now found it easier to credit him with similar feats during his long absence in the East.

ACROSS THE SAHARA IN QUEST OF NEGRO LANDS

It is possible that, while Ibn Battuta was away in the Negro lands, the return of other pilgrims who had been to Mecca brought verification of his reputation in faraway countries. Whatever happened to alter public opinion, the vizier became the wanderer's powerful supporter. He urged that the Commander of the Faithful, his master, must at once do everything possible to record the traveler's remarkable memories. As a consequence Sultan Abu Inan took steps to provide for him and assigned Ibn Juzayy, one of the principal royal secretaries, to write down the narrative.

Ibn Battuta was not a literary man, and what few notes he had set down were lost in his Indian misadventures. At the age of forty-nine he still possessed an extraordinary memory, trained early in life when he learned to recite the Koran by heart. He was not infallible, but he was able to recall names with almost 100 percent accuracy. Though he was doubtful of some oriental places, Ibn Juzayy carefully recorded them phonetically, so that many could be identified in later years.

It required some months for Ibn Battuta to organize his thoughts and plan what he would say. "Under the wing of the sultan's bounty," as he phrased it, he approached the project in a happy mood. At last his wanderings would take on substance and be of permanent worth. He was settled in a comfortable house and given a stipend while he worked at assembling his recollections of the preceding twenty-nine years. It took the best part of two years for the scribe to get his dictation down on paper. At first they went into past happenings in great detail, therefore the early parts of the narrative are the most complete. Ibn Juzayy seems to have wearied of the task toward the end, and he skimmed through the homeward journey from Sumatra and some of the Sahara Desert interludes. Perhaps he intended filling in the abridged portions later or maybe some other assignment or illness interfered. The explanation may lie in the fact that Ibn Juzayy died eight months after completing the book in December, 1355.

From then on Ibn Battuta's life was more serene than in

his footloose years. He terminated his career in the traditional way of his ancestors, as a revered judge in one of the Moroccan towns, dying in 1369 at the age of sixty-five. His burial place is unknown.

Several rare copies of his book found their way to libraries in Morocco and Spain. As they had been handwritten—there were no printing presses in that day—they were accessible only to scholars. When two Frenchmen discovered the volume in the 1880s and translated it from the Arabic text, the narrative threw light for the first time on a completely unknown period in some of the lands Ibn Battuta had visited. Knowledge of the world had increased by then, and there was no doubt that the Moor saw firsthand the sights he claimed to have witnessed. His book remains a monument to the inquiring mind of the medieval Arab who traveled farther than Marco Polo, covering what would have been an impressive distance even in the air age. He visited the countries of every Muslim ruler of his time, and at least three infidel realms—Byzantine Constantinople, Ceylon, and China. He defied illness, strange foods, bad weather, and dangerous men.

His admiring scribe could not help but append to the narrative when it was completed this tribute to Ibn Battuta:

It is plain to any man of intelligence that this sheikh is the traveler of the age; and if one were to say "the traveler par excellence of this our Muslim community" he would be guilty of no exaggeration.

Glossary

Ablutions.	The washing of face, hands, feet, and ears, required of Muslims before prayer.
Ambergris.	A waxy substance from the sperm whale used as a base in perfumery.
Arab.	In this book, a member of the Arabic-speaking nations as a whole—that is, a person whose native tongue was Arabic.
Baobab.	An African tree, with a huge central trunk, which bears edible fruit shape like gourds.
Bazaar.	A market or shopping street in Oriental countries.
Bedouins.	Wandering desert tribes of Arabia, Syria, and North Africa.
Berber.	A Muslim tribe of North Africa.
Betel.	A species of the pepper plant. Betel nut comes from the areca palm and is chewed in the East with lime and the leaves of the betel plant.
Brahman.	A member of the highest caste of India —descended from a family long distinguished for mental or spiritual superiority.

Breaking of the fast.	One of the two great Muslim festivals of the year. It is the end of Ramadan and coincides with the sighting of the new moon.
Caliph.	A temporal and spiritual Muslim ruler whose post was considered God-given. The first caliph was a companion of the Prophet. He appointed his successor, who shortly died. The third caliph, Ali, was the husband of Fatima, a daughter of the Prophet. The caliphate was supposedly a hereditary succession.
Calligraphy.	Handwritten script, usually very decorative. Since Islam frowned on reproductions of human figures, calligraphy was adapted to adornment of mosques and other religious buildings.
Couscous.	A food made in West Africa of baobab leaves, millet flour or rice, and meat.
Cowrie.	The shell of a small marine mollusk, used as money in Africa and the East Indies.
Dervish.	One of a group of men who lived in houses of meditation. Muhammad did not want monastic orders in Islam, but under the caliphs they sprang up, some with peculiar beliefs, finding exciting values in coffee-drinking, music, dancing, and beating themselves. The name means "threshold of a door."
Dinar.	One of the commonest gold coins of the Middle Ages. Those of Egypt and Syria may be taken as standard. They were worth roughly a little over $2.50.
Dirhem.	Twenty-five silver dirhems equaled one gold dinar.

GLOSSARY

Doctor of law.	One versed in Koranic law, another name for kadi.
Emir.	A prince, ruler, or military commander. It was a title of honor with various meanings.
Eunuch.	A man castrated in youth in order to obtain advancement at an Eastern court. For obvious reasons eunuchs made excellent harem officials and were frequently appointed to this post of honor. Some attained high government position under the rulers they served.
Grass cloth.	A fabric woven from tough grass or ramie fibers.
Hajj.	The pilgrimage to Mecca.
Hajji.	One who has made the pilgrimage to Mecca.
Hermitage.	An establishment of Muslim monks, dervishes, or religious brotherhoods of various natures. Often they were little more than rest houses for travelers.
Hodja.	The word means "master" or "teacher." Often he might also be a leader of public prayer and a magistrate.
Hospice.	A place of refuge for travelers, sometimes a lodging for the sick and poor.
Ibn Battuta.	This was the family's ancient name, but each son in a Muslim household was known by his own first name, followed by "ibn"—that is, "son of"—and then his father's name. When our man gave his full signature, he was Muhammad son of Abdalla son of Battuta.
Imam.	One appointed to lead prayers.
Infidel.	A non-Muslim.

Kaaba.

A cube-shaped granite structure in the inner courtyard of Mecca's Great Mosque —a building which was begun in the eighth century and now spreads over fifteen acres. The Kaaba stands alone and is draped in black brocade. The sacred black stone handed down from pagan times sits in its eastern corner.

Pilgrims make the circuit of the Kaaba seven times, repeating certain devotional phrases and kissing the black stone. Other parts of the pilgrimage ceremony include running seven times between two holy hills, washing at the well of Zamzam, and going twelve miles to the plain of Arafat, where all face Mecca and pray. Then on the tenth day stones are cast at three devil pillars, an animal is sacrificed, a feast is held, and the pilgrims again don their normal clothing.

Kadi.

A judge, all of whose decisions were based on interpretations of Muslim law as laid down by the Koran. (Similarly, in early colonial New England, all judging of misbehavior was based on the Bible's teachings, not on the common law.) A kadi's duties included examining disputes, enforcing judgments, administering estates of minors, supervising mosque property and schools, executing wills, imposing penalties for neglect of religious duties or refusal to pay taxes, and punishing crimes.

Khan.

A Chinese, Turkish, or Mongol title for a powerful ruler or chieftain.

Koran.

The Muslim holy book, as the Bible is to Christians and Jews. It was set forth by

	the Prophet Muhammad, to whom the Word of God was revealed by the Angel Gabriel. The Koran is four fifths as long as the New Testament.
Lateen sail.	A triangular sail extended by a long yard, slung to the mast about one-quarter distance from the sail's lower end.
Millet.	The seed of a grass cultivated in the Old World in ancient times as a cereal. In our country it is regarded as a forage plant.
Minaret.	The tall, slender tower of a mosque, having a circular balcony from which the call to prayer could be delivered. From this high vantage point, a muezzin could be heard far and wide. Often a mosque had several minarets.
Miskal.	A gold or silver coin.
Moor.	A native of Morocco.
Morocco.	In the fourteenth century this was known as the Maghrib, or West, but the author has used the more familiar name.
Muezzin.	A crier who mounts a minaret and calls people to prayer.
Muslim calendar.	Muslims date all events A.H. (After the Hegira), beginning in the Christian year 622. The author has not employed the Muslim calendar except in relation to Ramadan.
Night of Power.	The most important date in Ramadan, the twenty-seventh of the month. It commemorates the handing down of the Koran from Heaven. Devout Muslims believe that this was the time when all divine decrees for the following years are issued.
Palanquin.	A covered conveyance used in the Orient,

usually for one person. It is carried on poles.

Pasha. A high civil or military official.

Pilgrimage. The annual journey to Mecca organized in various parts of the Muslim world. Most travelers eventually joined the enormous caravans leaving Cairo, Damascus, and Baghdad, but they began in smaller units assembled in remote places and united with the larger caravans for protection. Usually the pilgrimage was made in the twelfth month of the Muslim year.

The pilgrimage is regarded as the ideal culmination of religious experience. To this day it attracts about 750,000 pilgrims annually, about a third of them coming from foreign lands. A large percentage arrive at the port of Jidda, forty-five miles from Mecca, which can be reached by air as well as water. However, although modern pilgrims fly to Jidda, they must cover the final miles to Mecca by camel, car, bus, or on foot. They still shed their shoes and don pilgrim garb the last part of the way.

Ramadan. The month of fasting in the Muslim calendar, when the believer does not eat or seek pleasure from sunup to sundown.

Sanctuary. A holy place usually honoring a sainted person.

Seven Wonders of the Ancient World. The pyramids of Egypt; the gardens of Semiramis at Babylon; the statue of Jupiter at Olympia; the temple of Diana at Ephesus; the mausoleum at Halicarnassus; the Colossus of Rhodes; and the Pharos at Alexandria.

GLOSSARY

Shah.	A Persian term for ruler.
Sharif.	A descendant of Muhammad.
Sheikh.	A venerable man or the head of a tribe or one of the higher order of religious persons entitled to preach in a mosque.
Sinhalese.	Natives of Ceylon.
Sultan.	A Muslim civil ruler, similar to a king in medieval Europe.
Tamarind.	A tropical tree with a flat brown pod containing an acid pulp.
Tanga.	Either a gold or silver coin issued by Muslim rulers in the East. The Portuguese in India issued a copper coin by that name, valued at one tenth of a rupee.
Tatar.	A Turkish tribesman from the Crimea or other specific parts of Asia.
Turkoman.	A Turk originating in what are today the Turkmen, Uzbek, and Kazakh Soviet republics.
Vizier.	A minister of state, the ruler's chief counselor.
Yogi.	One who practices complete concentration on something, especially the deity, for the purpose of achieving a mystic state.

Index

INDEX

INDEX

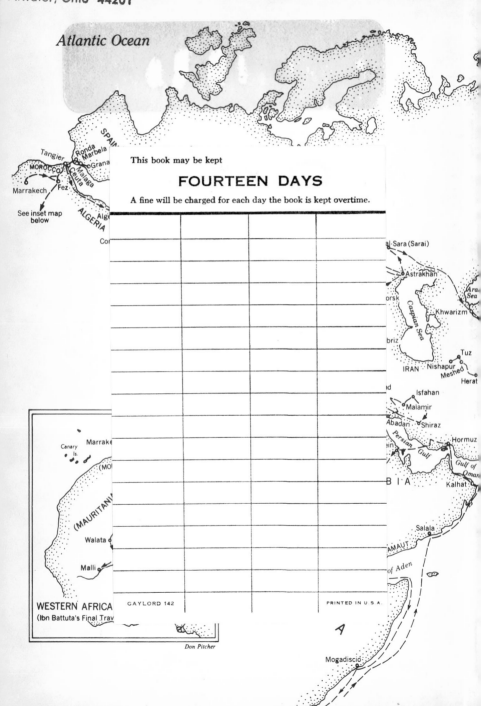

Atlantic Ocean

This book may be kept

FOURTEEN DAYS

A fine will be charged for each day the book is kept overtime.

GAYLORD 142

PRINTED IN U.S.A.

Don Pitcher